Kindred Spirits

KINDRED SPIRITS

Developing Godly Friendships

Kathy Narramore
Alice Hill

PYRANEE BOOKS

Zondervan Publishing House
Grand Rapids, Michigan

Pyranee Books are published by Zondervan Publishing House,
1415 Lake Drive, S.E., Grand Rapids, Michigan 49506.

KINDRED SPIRITS
COPYRIGHT © 1985 BY THE ZONDERVAN CORPORATION
GRAND RAPIDS, MICHIGAN

Library of Congress Cataloging in Publication Data

Narramore, Kathy.
   Kindred spirits.

"Pyranee books."
   1. Friendship—Religious aspects—Christianity. 2. Christian life—
1960-   . I. Hill, Alice. II. Title.
BV4647.F7N36   1985   248.4   85-10787

ISBN 0-310-30531-4

All rights reserved. No part of this publication may be reproduced, stored in a retrieval system, or transmitted in any form or by any means without the prior permission of the publisher.

Unless otherwise indicated, Scripture quotations are from the HOLY BIBLE: NEW INTERNATIONAL VERSION (North American Edition). Copyright © 1978 by the International Bible Society. Used by permission of Zondervan Bible Publishers.

Printed in the United States of America

85 86 87 88 89 90 91 92 / 10 9 8 7 6 5 4 3 2 1

To our husbands whose love and humor kept us going—

Bruce who edited

Dick who supported the editor

and to those special friends who never gave up on us or this book. Your love, prayers, support, typing, and editing are deeply appreciated.

Contents

—— Part One ——
The Lifestyle of Godly Friendships

1. But I Already Have God! 15
2. Some of Jesus' Friends 19
3. I Accept You, I Understand 31
4. I Care, I Forgive, I'll Pray With You 41
5. I Will Comfort and Encourage You 53
6. I Will Lovingly Confront You 59
7. You—God's Mirror to Me 75

—— Part Two ——
What Godly Friendships Will Mean to Me

8. How Do I Feel? 89
9. Do We Dare? 97
10. Let's Begin! 111
    Study Questions 123

Preface

While the idea of a biblical friendship was a new one to us at first, we eventually realized we had rediscovered an historical lifestyle. It was a trademark of the early church which met together daily sharing not only their worship but their food, money, and their very lives (Acts 2:44–47). But it was this togetherness that brought them persecution.

The Romans could not understand why this new sect held meetings all the time—even daily. Why could they not go singly, or in families, to the temples and make offerings to their god, and then come away, as the pagans did? In his book, *Systematic Theology*, A. H. Strong said, "It was the natural and inevitable expression of their union with Christ and so of their union with one another."

Then came the "dark ages" of the church's life, ended by Martin Luther's call for reform and a return to the Bible. A hundred years later much of the church was pure in its doctrine but dead in its inner life. Deeply concerned, a young minister in Frankfort, Germany, Philip Spener, began to meet with a small group of people in his home. From this came the idea of circles of people in each local

Kindred Spirits

church meeting for the purposes of Bible study and helping each other materially and spiritually.

Out of this movement rose the Moravian founder, Count Zinzendorf, the first man to light the torch of Protestant missionary zeal, sending out his people to spread the gospel to all parts of the world.

About a hundred years after Spener, England was growing in wealth and power but the church was stagnant and corrupt. In 1738, a young minister, John Wesley, and his brother, Charles, were led to a "heartwarming" experience through the influence of the deeply spiritual Moravians. Through the preaching of John Wesley, England and America experienced the "Great Awakening," a spiritual revival that transformed the whole of English life. Much of the ignorance, coarseness, brutality, and drunkenness of English life disappeared. Christians led the way in prison reform, the abolition of slavery, and the establishment and growth of Sunday schools.

In this unprecedented expression of spiritual life and power, what was the lifestyle of the church? For the most part they were meeting regularly in small groups for the purpose of caring for and encouraging one another. Here they experienced a high level of trust and mutual commitment. This created the climate in which they practiced the kind of caring called for in the "each other" commands. "Only by the disclosure of the interior life," wrote one of the Methodist leaders, could there be congruency between the outward expression and inward experience of the Christian life. When there is honest self disclosure in a mutual, caring climate, then "only are we prepared to comfort, encourage and strengthen one another" (*Class Meetings,* Leonidas Rosser.)

What about today? Many are praying again for another "great awakening" of spiritual empowering. If ever there was a need for Christians to live what they believe, it

Preface

is now, and the land will be healed as we confess our sins not only to the Lord but to those who are our Kindred Spirits—those who share our basic beliefs and attitudes and who through their love and concern for us will prod us on toward godliness. We can return to personal holiness and Christlikeness by developing a biblical lifestyle of mutual care and accountability. This will not get easier as our culture becomes further estranged from Christian values and biblical moorings, and such a return will cost us. Yet we invite you to look at what biblical friendships could mean to you—what they will cost and the incredible rewards they will pay.

Alice and Kathy

— *Part One* —

THE LIFESTYLE OF GODLY FRIENDSHIPS

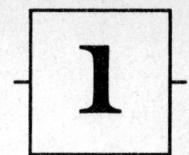

BUT I ALREADY HAVE GOD!

A few years ago if we had been asked, "Why do we need a close friend when we already have God?" we would have individually replied, "We don't." God was all we needed. Scripture itself told us that His grace was sufficient, that we were to cast our cares on Him, and that we were to come unto *Him* who would give us rest. So we took our needs and problems to God—it didn't seem right to admit spiritual needs to anyone else.

Neither did it seem right to ask for help from others, so we focused on giving help *to* others to encourage their growth in the Christian life. By ministering to others we were on the well-marked path toward Christian maturity, or so we thought.

God alone and our service for Him seemed to meet our personal needs until we married. Within the walls of our homes, the joy we had experienced ministering to others seemed to vanish like water into vapor.

Alice entered marriage expecting Dick to meet all her needs. She remembers those early years well.

Kindred Spirits

Coming from a divorced home, I subconsciously wanted Dick to make up for my past feelings of hurt, rejection and lack of self worth. When he failed, I felt extremely let down and angry. My constant demands kept him always on the defensive and me, feeling like a nag. Then I'd get angry with myself for having needs.

I wasn't the mother I wanted to be either. I questioned how I could be such a warm and loving Christian toward the teenagers in my Bible study and at the same time struggle with such intense anger toward my daughter. I felt like two people inside—Maria of the *Sound of Music* and the witch in the *Wizard of Oz*.

Kathy also struggled through those early years of marriage, feeling Bruce was the only human she could allow to meet all her needs.

I wanted him to be perfect, and therefore, when he failed to live up to all my ideals, I looked down on him just as far as I had, previously looked up at him. Either way, I kept him at a distance.

Marriage revealed a capacity for anger—both the volcanic and iceberg varieties—that shocked me. I'd rehearse retaliatory speeches as I did breakfast dishes after Bruce had left in the morning, but such thoughts didn't come without knots forming in my stomach. *How can this be*, I'd think, *when I've married the most wonderful man in the world—and my own personal psychologist at that?*

In our second year of marriage our son, Dickie, was born. In the next few months, between moving, entertaining, and speaking, I exceeded my strength and grew increasingly exhausted, cutting everything but routine tasks out of my schedule. One might call my experience a full-fledged identity crisis—going from career to wife and mother. As my ministry went out the window so did my assurance of my value to God.

Motherhood further complicated my life nearly three years later when our daughter Debbie arrived. As she and Dickie grew older I became more aware of my inadequacies as a mother. I'd hear my own condemning tones rerun when Dickie would get mad at Debbie or when they would hit each other in retaliation the way I'd spank them when I was angry.

But I Already Have God!

Each of us took these matters to God—often. But under the stress we also began talking to each other about them.

We had been meeting together once a month after renewing a friendship that had begun in college. Each time we met we found it easy to share our spiritual lives and our ministries. Within a few months we began letting each other into the more disquieting areas of our personal lives, talking about how things really were at home, what we *really* said and did, not just what we *should* do and say. Being with each other once a month was like finding water in the desert because we felt understood and accepted. We always left each other's company with more love to give our families than when we had arrived.

But this comfort and growth was sabotaged by guilt. We felt guilty for spending time together instead of spending that time alone with God praying and reading the Bible, or spending that time witnessing to people who didn't even know Him. The only purpose we saw for being with other Christians was to help those who were more needy than we. It never occurred to us that God might want us to minister to each other.

We felt guilty about needing each other. Nobody else seemed to need other people to help them grow. Having always believed the Bible to be the chief source of God's love, comfort, and correction, we didn't need each other, or did we?

But we didn't just seem to *need* each other, we enjoyed each other's company. We shared meaningful Scripture passages, deep thoughts, good books, lots of telephone calls, a love for Chinese food, and laughter.

The longer we were friends the more evident it became that we were truly kindred spirits. In addition to the many beliefs, attitudes, and feelings we shared, we found that we were alike in many other ways. Neither of us is satisfied with what appears on the surface; we have a need to dig, analyze, and uncover. We find it hard to settle for "what is," but strive for "what can be." Therefore, we faced our conflicts in much the same way. We weren't willing just to stay the way we were, declaring our problems to be "our cross to bear." Both of us sincerely wanted to change but we didn't know how. We tried to apply the Scriptures we read and the scriptural formulas we knew but our efforts only brought temporary help. The doctrines in our heads somehow weren't touching the deep needs in our hearts. But why?

Our commitment to the authority of God's Word—rather than to experiences or to what we'd always thought—prompted us to begin digging into the Word, hoping to discover some answers. We were shocked when we found that much of what we'd always thought was unbiblical.

2

SOME OF JESUS' FRIENDS

The answer began to unfold with the discovery of just two little words—"each other." After years of reading the Bible we discovered these words. We'd clearly understood our need for God, but suddenly we were jarred with verses telling us we also needed each other to bear our burdens, to hear our confessions, to encourage us, to build us up, to love us fervently.

These verses called us to each other within the body of Christ, and they described a lifestyle of relating we had not taken seriously in terms of our friendship with each other.

Throughout our Christian lives we had looked to Jesus' attributes to direct our inner growth and character; we knew we were to become like Him. But we had looked with tunnel vision. Now we expanded our sights to take in His relationships.

What were Jesus' relationships like? What attitudes did He have toward people? Everywhere He went people were drawn to Him. Multitudes were always in desperate need of His presence and care. But He seemed to have invested

Kindred Spirits

an extraordinary amount of time caring and being concerned for twelve carefully chosen men, His disciples.

We wondered what kind of relationship Jesus had with these men. We knew He was their Master-Teacher and loving Leader, but we had not taken seriously His friendship with them. In John 15:15 He calls them His friends.

It was Jesus' friendships we wanted to observe more carefully. How would His friendship fit in with His goal of preparing them to usher in His new kingdom in just three years? How would it help Him take ignorant, narrow-minded, superstitious men who were full of Jewish prejudices, misconceptions, and animosities, and transform them into ardent apostles of salvation?

Jesus lived His life in increasingly intimate circles of friendship. With the multitude He was the least intimate. With the Twelve, He lived day and night, sharing His spiritual insights and struggles. Within the Twelve there was a smaller group who knew Jesus more personally—Peter, James, and John. To only these three Jesus revealed the fullness of His glory on the Mount of Transfiguration and the depths of His suffering in Gethsemane. There were also close friends outside the Twelve who shared His inner circle—Lazarus, Mary, and Martha.

Apparently Jesus had one most intimate relationship. This was with John, the only one He called His "beloved disciple."

Since John and Peter were part of the "inner circle" and since they appeared to have had an intimacy with each other (their names are often linked), we focused on their friendship with Jesus. Both John and Peter were fishermen, activists, and daring. Yet they were radically different personalities. Peter was generous, frank, and sometimes impulsive. John was more constant, often rigid, and explosive.

Some of Jesus' Friends

The Beloved Disciple

Jesus appropriately named John the Son of Thunder. One day while Jesus, James, and John were traveling to Jerusalem, Jesus sent James and John, who were brothers, ahead to make reservations. When they arrived, they were told by bigoted Samaritans that there was no room. In impulsive anger John and James asked, "Lord, do you want us to command fire to come down from heaven and consume them?" But Jesus turned and rebuked them, and he said, "You do not know what kind of spirit you are of; for the Son of Man did not come to destroy men's lives, but to save them" (Luke 9:54–55 NAS). Jesus quickly redirected James' and John's attention from the rejecting Samaritans to the raging intolerance in their own hearts. James and John, like most of us, found it easier to look at the Samaritans' problems than their own. Yet Jesus firmly switched the focus to their own unloving attitudes. It was like holding up a mirror so the brothers could see themselves as they really were.

We read another incident. This time the mother of John and James sought acquire honor and position for her sons in Jesus' kingdom. As a good Jewish mother she spoke for John and James, saying, "Grant that one of these two sons of mine may sit at your right and the other at your left in your kingdom" (Matthew 20:21). It was as if she were saying, "Now that my sons are in Your inner circle we want to guarantee they will get special honor and position when You take over. After all, isn't that the privilege of being Your right-hand man?" Perhaps John and his mother and brother wanted to use their friendship with Jesus to obtain prestige for themselves, even if it meant pushing others, including Peter, aside.

Jesus answered, "You don't know what you are asking.... To sit at my right or left is not for me to grant.

Kindred Spirits

These places belong to those for whom they have been prepared.... You know that those who are regarded as rulers of the Gentiles lord it over them, and their high officials exercise authority over them. Not so with you. Instead, whoever wants to become great among you must be your servant, and whoever wants to be first must be slave of all. For even the Son of Man did not come to be served, but to serve, and to give his life as a ransom for many" (Mark 10:38–45).

This interaction brought home John's distorted views of friendship. John wanted to be served and favored, while Jesus wanted John to know a true friend was one who gladly serves. Jesus did not view closeness as a way of gaining advantage over others. For Him closeness was a means of equipping and encouraging—not improving status. Instead of going along with John's request or angrily rebuking him, Jesus lovingly corrected by His own example of humility.

When we looked at the context of the timing of John's request, we realized how much John had to learn about himself and about Jesus. Jesus had just been explaining to the disciples that He was on His way to Jerusalem to be tortured and killed when John's mother asked if her sons could be favored! Think of the contrast. The Son of God is about to go through an agonizing death for a lost world, and James and John are thinking about ensuring a throne for themselves. Their own selfishness deafened them to Jesus' words and feelings. John could see neither his selfishness nor Christ's agony. And since John didn't see his own sin, he wasn't looking for One to take it away. He didn't want a cross, but a crown.

Once again Jesus stepped in to show John more about Himself. He didn't condemn John, but firmly let him know that prestige was not a concern of His! And by the end of that day John had probably learned more about himself

Some of Jesus' Friends

and Jesus' disconcerting love than he would have from any number of lectures or sermons. He had experienced Jesus' love in action. And after the trauma of Calvary you can be sure John finally understood both the depths of his own selfishness and his need for the total unselfishness of Christ's love.

Perhaps one verse highlights some of the changes that took place in John's life. "When they had testified and proclaimed the word of the Lord, Peter and John returned to Jerusalem, preaching the gospel in many Samaritan villages" (Acts 8:25). Here we see John returning to the very place of his murderous anger, bigotry, and intolerance. But now he was a new person with new attitudes toward these Samaritans and a new message of humility and hope. He had received needed forgiveness and new life and wanted to share it with them. Gone was his selfish ambition, his competitiveness, his demand for exclusive favor. He was even on this mission with Peter—the very one he had formerly tried to edge out for a special place in the kingdom! And by the time we get to John's Epistles we see that the formerly angry Son of Thunder has been tempered and changed to become the Apostle of Love. Three years of not just listening to Jesus but being with Him—watching the expressions of His face, catching His tone of voice, experiencing His firm but loving correction, witnessing the crucifixion and experiencing the power of the resurrection—had revolutionized his life.

An Impulsive Fisherman

Then there was Peter—a commercial fisherman in partnership with John. Like John, Peter was looking more for a strong political deliverer than for the Son of God who would take away his sin. He too had some serious misconceptions about himself and Jesus. One day as Jesus was preaching to the crowds on the lakeshore, He noticed two empty fishing boats. He asked Simon Peter, the owner of one, to row Him out a short distance so He could better speak to the crowds on the shore. When He had finished speaking, Jesus called to Simon, the owner of the boat, "Put out into deep water, and let down the nets for a catch."

Simon answered, "Master, we've worked hard all night and haven't caught anything. But because you say so, I will let down the nets."

This time their nets came up so full that they began to tear! A shout for help brought His partner, John. Both boats were so filled with fish they were on the verge of sinking. When Simon Peter realized what had happened, he fell to his knees before Jesus and said, "Go away from me, Lord; I am a sinful man!" (Luke 5:4–8).

As we studied the passage we wondered if Peter could have been thinking to himself, *Here is a miracle if I've ever seen one—and in this occupation I ought to know! How incredulous is this Man's power, and to think He'd used it to help me! But I don't deserve this kind of concern. He doesn't really know or understand me. He's too good and great to be around me . . . if He only knew what I was really like.* So Peter said, "Go away from me, Lord, I'm too much of a sinner."

Peter had probably stereotyped Jesus as being like the other religious leaders who separated themselves from the people with their show of false righteousness. Maybe Peter didn't want Jesus to come too close because he feared His disappointment or condemnation. But Peter was understood even though he did not understand. Jesus said, "Don't be afraid; from now on you will catch men" (Luke 5:10). This last statement must have really jolted Peter's perception of himself and Jesus. Here was Jesus the Son of God, understanding him rather than condemning him and then telling an unstable, easily swayed, and inconsistent fisherman that he would play a key role in Jesus' ministry.

Some of Jesus' Friends

Jesus wisely didn't tell Peter the whole story—that he would become Peter the rock, the one who would help turn the world upside down with His Good News and be faithful to Christ even to death. This would surely have been more than Peter could have handled! What great sensitivity Jesus showed—to come to Peter and use fishing, which Peter understood best, to reveal what he understood least—himself and his God. Jesus was building trust so that He could meet Peter's deeper spiritual and emotional needs, and helping Peter see himself more accurately.

As great as were Peter's initial self-doubts, Jesus' understanding, acceptance, and miraculous power persuaded him to leave everything and follow Him. Yet Peter's doubts weren't over—especially as portrayed one night on the Sea of Galilee.

Jesus had instructed the disciples to go out to sea without Him, but seeing they were struggling against a storm, He walked on the water out to them. Instead of crying, "Oh Jesus, we knew You'd come," they screamed in panic, thinking it was a ghost. Once more Jesus assured Peter and the others, "Take courage! It is I. Don't be afraid."

The others believed, but Peter wasn't satisfied with mere belief. Swinging from utter fear to reckless presumption he cried, "Lord, if it's You, tell me to come to You on the water." But the pressure of the situation revealed how unsure of Jesus Peter really was, and he began sinking. Jesus didn't overlook his doubt. He pinpointed it by asking, "You of little faith, why did you doubt?" (Matthew 14:27–31). At the same time He extended His hand and rescued Peter. Jesus was a sensitive, patient friend; yet He never encouraged denial of what was going on around or within a person.

Peter had other "falls" before his trust in Jesus' love and commitment grew to that of the mighty preacher of

Kindred Spirits

Pentecost—rock-like in his faith. Because of his limited understanding of both Christ and himself he had a habit of "rushing in where angels fear to tread." He tried to manage other people's lives, including Christ's. And he was a master at offering unneeded or incorrect advice before he understood the situation. Regarding the necessity and ordeal of Christ's coming death, Peter took Him aside and "rebuked" Him: "'Never, Lord!' he said. 'This shall never happen to you!'" (Matthew 16:22). And during the Last Supper when Jesus was washing the disciples' feet, Peter incredulously asked, "Lord, are you going to wash my feet?" When Jesus said, "You do not realize now what I am doing, but later you will understand," Peter proudly replied, "No, you shall never wash my feet." Finally, Jesus decided to cut through Peter's brashness and misunderstanding of humility. He firmly but lovingly told him, "Unless I wash you, you have no part with me." And then Peter got the message. But true to his impulsive style he said, "Then, Lord, not just my feet but my hands and my head as well!" (John 13:6–9).

Jesus didn't treat Peter with disdain or distrust because he wasn't mature enough to understand fully either Jesus' mission or his own brashness. Jesus accepted him as he was and firmly led him on to where he needed to be, demonstrating infinite humility by His actions and His manner—the very qualities Peter so desperately needed.

Still, a sense of stability and maturity did not come easily to Peter. When Jesus warned the disciples that they would desert Him, Peter confidently declared, "Even if all fall away, I will not" (Mark 14:29). But a short time later his fear of man's disapproval prompted him to deny he even knew Jesus (Mark 14:68). Yet Jesus' friendship and unfailing commitment remained true to him. Catching Jesus' look of pain, understanding, and forgiveness as He was being led away, Peter grieved and wept bitter tears. He saw how he had rejected his dearest friend, the Son of God. Humility finally came because he recognized the extent of his sin reflected in his instability, brashness, and disloyalty and because he repeatedly saw and experienced the firm committed example of Christ. Unlike Judas, whose remorse caused him to go out and hang himself, Peter was healed by receiving and experiencing Jesus' full acceptance and forgiveness.

Both John's and Peter's lives were revolutionized because Jesus helped them see themselves and Himself more clearly. They learned to overcome their fears of being rejected and their desires for special privileges by facing realistically their own sinfulness and the loving faithfulness of Christ. He confronted them with their sins but graciously forgave them. He was patiently committed to them and humbly cared for their needs as He slowly showed them they could trust Him. They both observed His reactions to themselves and to others, and they witnessed the depths of His caring. They saw Him moved to compassion over the plight of a leper, a deaf and speechless man, the crowds of harassed, helpless people. They saw Him weep in grief with Mary over the loss of her brother, Lazarus.

They saw not only Christ's compassion but His unique power—to heal the handicapped, to feed the physically and spiritually hungry, and to raise the dead. Jesus' disciples had become far more to Him than servants carrying out orders. They had become His closest friends. He did not just teach them about His love, they experienced it through their friendships with Him.

Jesus' New Command

After three years of living with Jesus, seeing His face, hearing His voice, receiving His total understanding and caring, you can imagine the shock and sorrow the disciples suffered when Jesus told them He was going to leave them.

Kindred Spirits

During the meal Jesus poured water into a basin and began to wash His disciples' feet (John 13). Tenderly He performed this humble task for each disciple—including Judas who would soon betray Him. Then, waiting until Judas left, He shared His deepest concern: "A new command I give you: Love one another. As I have loved you, so you must love one another. By this all men will know that you are my disciples, if you love one another" (John 13:34–35).

"Love—as I have loved you." With what depth of feeling the disciples must have heard those words as the memories of all their experiences of His love came flooding back. Yet here was a new provision for them. In His absence they were to offer His kind of love to each other. Not only would they *give* His manner of love to each other, they would also receive it and experience it. Their love for each other would make His love tangible to each other and His love visible to the world.

That last night intimate friendship, which loves the way God loves, was God's provision for eleven grieving disciples. And it is the same gracious provision for those of us indwelt by Him today. It is as if Jesus were saying to each of us, "You will experience my love as you love each other. You can know about my love from my Word but you are to experience it through your friendships. This will be possible not only because I will be with you, but because I will be *in* you, through my Spirit empowering you."

It seems God planned for us to do our spiritual and emotional maturing in relationships with others. Growth takes place in context of relationships. Christian friendships are designed to promote our growth toward maturity by helping us see God and ourselves. They can also help meet our deep emotional needs as we accept, care for, encourage, forgive, and are committed to one another. As we do this for one another we reflect the Lord to one another.

Some of Jesus' Friends

Therefore we call this kind of friendship "godly" friendship.

Now that we understood the quality and purpose of godly friendship we wanted to find out more about how these friendships were to function. We wanted to know the different facets of this kind of friendship God intended for us. In the following chapters we will take a closer look at a few of them.

3

I ACCEPT YOU, I UNDERSTAND

We began our study of the "each others" by examining this command to accept one another. As we studied the context of this verse we realized that biblical acceptance is not simply a nice social thing to offer one another. According to Paul, acceptance is a means of glorifying God!

This immediately set us thinking further: How does God accept us? What are the results of His acceptance? The most obvious characteristic of God's acceptance is that it is unconditional—or perhaps we should say *one* conditional. Some people who talk of unconditional acceptance ignore the fact that we mortals are sinful, and they act as if there are no real barriers to God's acceptance of us or our acceptance of each other. We should accept each other, they say, "just because we exist!" But according to the Bible, our sin has erected such a barrier between ourselves and God that God can't accept us unless this barrier is removed. This *one* condition is that we acknowledge our sinfulness and appropriate Christ's payment for it. On this

Kindred Spirits

basis God takes us *un*conditionally—exactly as we are. And because of this we can accept each other. But that is easier said than done! It is easier to accept some people than others, and it is easier to accept close friends and family on a conditional basis: We accept you when you do as we wish.

Accepting people we only know casually is usually easy. But it is difficult when we encounter flaws or habits or characteristics that touch us personally! As we looked at our own lives we found that, rather than accepting others as Christ does, we often responded to their imperfections or sinful traits with criticism, alienation, anxiety, or even contempt. We often failed to accept others the way Christ accepted John and Peter and the way He accepts us. Yet we longed to experience this kind of acceptance from other people and to learn to accept them without judging or criticizing.

Feeling Accepted by Others

As our friendship deepened we began to understand the reason we had difficulty accepting others: We hadn't really felt accepted. We needed to experience acceptance ourselves if we were to be able to offer it to others.

Alice, having grown up in a single-parent home, was extremely sensitive to rejection, and she remembers her struggles well:

> I had convinced myself that God would accept me when I lived up to His expectations and that others would do the same. This strong need for approval often motivated my giving to others. Running on a wearisome treadmill, I tried to earn from others what had already been given me by my heavenly Father as a gift—acceptance and approval.
>
> When I started realizing the tremendous pressure I was putting on myself, I searched the Scripture to find out more about God's love and acceptance of me. In Ephesians 1:4–5 I read that in love I was,

I Accept You, I Understand

before the creation of the world, predestined to be His adopted child in accordance with His pleasure. I was no longer condemned, being in Jesus Christ (Romans 8:1), and I was declared perfect in His eyes and welcome in His presence any time—no matter how well or poorly I performed (Hebrews 4:15). I wanted to feel assurance of God's promises. The verses gave me a new sense of value and directed me toward experiencing Christ's acceptance. I knew my old way of giving out love to get back love was not Christ's way of experiencing acceptance.

The day after I read these verses I was slinging the vacuum up and down the hall like super-woman, but feeling like a helpless child inside. My strong appearing exterior and inner weakness seemed to collide, and, above the blare of the Kirby, I blurted out, "Lord, please, . . . I need help."

God didn't respond verbally, but I knew I could turn to Kathy and lean on her as I faced the problems within myself, with Dick, and with our children. Kathy had accepted what she already knew about me, so I began letting her into more troublesome areas of my life. As she accepted me, I became more aware of the meaning of the words in the Scriptures that had seemed so vague. Kathy's acceptance was Christ's way for me to experience His acceptance. Kathy was like Him in that the more she knew about me the more she accepted me. Intimacy didn't bring rejection.

But the need for acceptance wasn't only Alice's. When Kathy began to see the freedom Alice was experiencing as she faced herself, Kathy began to want that for herself.

Having mainly shared with Alice my struggles within my ministry, I admitted few of my real struggles at home. Alice had been understanding and encouraging; she'd accepted my shortcomings, but I was afraid she wouldn't want me for a friend if she knew what I was really like at home. One day I acknowledged that I did not accept Bruce's and my children's shortcomings as readily as almost everyone else's, and I described how often I lashed out or withdrew from them when they acted in ways I deemed unacceptable.

At first Alice didn't take Kathy's struggle too seriously because it seemed so contrary to the Kathy she knew—confident, put together, always smiling. Alice remembers,

Kindred Spirits

> There was a part of me that didn't want to hear about Kathy's problems, because I had enough of my own to cope with, and I didn't want Kathy, who had been the one I leaned on, to be as weak as I felt.

But we continued to share and listen to each other, accepting whatever we heard. Within this accepting climate we could be honest rather than defensive and let in the acceptance and love—from each other and from God—which we both needed.

Accepting Others

The more we experience acceptance from others, the more acceptance we can offer to others.

Kathy remembers when this awareness hit her.

> One day our five-year-old son, Dickie, had been into all sorts of trouble. As usual, I had lost my temper and scolded him angrily. All of a sudden, as I was turning the corner of the hall, I realized how harshly I had treated him, and how hurt he must feel! I felt terribly guilty and ashamed. Then I heard another voice within and realized that at that very moment God was accepting—not rejecting me—just as I was. Tears came to my eyes as I sensed the depth of His forgiving, accepting love, and immediately my attitude toward Dickie changed. I went to his room, apologized for my attitude, and was able to communicate how much I loved him even when he misbehaved.
>
> Later when I reflected on this experience I realized why I had been able to feel accepted and get over my anger so quickly. I had been sharing my struggle with my temper with Alice and a couple of other close friends who loved me in spite of my anger. Their acceptance was helping God's acceptance become real to me, so I could offer the same kind of love to Dickie.

When we can offer others acceptance rather than judgment we create a godly climate in which to grow. Condemnation can produce behavior changes, but not healthy personality change, because it motivates out of fear and guilt, which is not God's method of promoting change. In fact, when we are condemned we may sin more, reacting defensively or lashing back. When we are accepted we sin less. Accepting each other not only helps us grow more holy because we are being more like Him, but it makes real God's acceptance of us. Deep personality change can come as we experience God's unconditional acceptance reflected through His people.

Empathize with One Another

As we were learning the importance of acceptance we came across a passage describing the depth of our reactions to each other: "Rejoice with those who rejoice; mourn with those who mourn" (Romans 12:15). Shedding further light on the qualities of godly friendship, is Hebrews 4:15 (KJV): "For we have not a high priest which cannot be touched with the feeling of our infirmities; but was in all points tempted like as we are, yet without sin."

Jesus is touched with the *feelings* of our infirmities. He doesn't simply have an intellectual awareness of our problems and struggles, but He is able to step into our shoes and experience the struggles we are having. This is the empathy we are to emulate.

Nothing touches our feelings of loneliness or the gloom of rejection like a friend who understands our feelings and reflects that understanding. Empathy helps us feel cared for, loved, and understood.

In his book *Why Am I Afraid to Tell You Who I Am?* John Powell says,

> . . . no one can really love us effectively unless he really understands us. Anyone who feels that he is understood, however, will certainly feel that he is loved.
>
> If there is no one who understands me, and who accepts me for what I am, I will feel "estranged." My talents and possessions will not comfort me at all. Even in the midst of many people, I will always carry within me a feeling of isolation and aloneness. I will experience a kind of "solitary confinement." It is a law as certain as the law of

Kindred Spirits

> gravity, that he who is understood and loved will grow as a person: he who is estranged will die in his cell of solitary confinement, alone (pp. 95–96).

Because we are part of the body of Christ we are to identify closely with each other and enter into each other's pain and joy as though it were happening to us. The Living Bible paraphrases Romans 12:15 slightly differently: "When others are happy, be happy with them. If they are sad, share their sorrow." That's often easier said than done. It can be a struggle to enter into another's sorrow, especially if we have difficulty accepting pain and sadness within ourselves. Bev, a mutual friend of ours, shared with her Sunday School class a crisis her daughter was facing. While Bev was talking she began to cry and the group then prayed for her. After class one woman approached Bev, briskly patting her on the back, and said, "Cheer up. Everything is going to be all right. Just trust God. He's going to heal her." Another woman came up and quietly said, "Bev, I really know how hard it must be for you to see your daughter go through so much pain." Bev again began to cry. She reached out to the woman and threw her arms around her. Confident that she was understood, she knew she was no longer alone. The first woman's optimism and spiritual concern masked her inability to really empathize and understand. She was apparently so uncomfortable with her friend's pain that she quickly had to pass it off with a "spiritual" solution. Proverbs describes the problem: "Being happy-go-lucky around a person whose heart is heavy is as bad as stealing his jacket in cold weather, or rubbing salt in his wounds" (25:20, LB). It can also be difficult to be happy with others when it appears God is blessing them more than us. Others' fortune can bring out our jealousy and envy, our resentment of God's goodness to them rather than our joy at their blessing.

Some friends of ours had a hard time finding people

who could share their celebration when they bought a new car. The day they got it they felt hesitant to call their friends because they remembered previous experiences. When they had related some of their blessings of good fortune and fame with them, their friends had responded with silence or disinterest, instead of with joy. Our friends summed up their experience by saying, "You know I think if we had an accident and totaled our car, these friends would gladly share our sorrow."

For many years our reactions to our husbands moods or behavior were often inappropriate or unhelpful. When our husbands appeared quiet or passive we grew angry or independent. We felt lonely and abandoned when they became depressed or preoccupied. But when we identified our desires to offer our husbands acceptance and empathy instead of anger, we committed ourselves to helping each other grow out of these old, programmed reactions. We helped each other by empathically listening and carefully offering insight without ever taking sides against the other's husband, saying, "Oh, poor you!"

Ways of Offering Empathy

Reflecting on our growing empathy for and acceptance of not only our husbands and children but each other, we identified what allowed us to empathize with each other. As we've said, until we understood and accepted ourselves it was hard to understand and accept others. But we also had learned the importance of *careful listening*. If we are too quick to rush in to comfort a friend by giving advice we can actually communicate a lack of understanding. Even scriptural advice can interfere with empathy if offered at the wrong moment, because it can reinforce how far short of God's standard the friend has fallen instead of lifting her up. Proverbs 15:23 says, "How good is a timely word!"

Kindred Spirits

One day while in a restaurant we overheard two apparently Christian men talking over lunch. One began to describe his wife's severe illness, his own lack of faith for her improvement, his resentment, and his dread of the future. The other man responded, "Praise the Lord! You should begin just praising Him, Walt, for all you are going to learn through this."

The tragedy was not that the man with the sick wife was not "growing" but that his friend was not with him in his pain. Walt's friend had failed to reflect our High Priest who can be touched with the feelings of our infirmities as well as overcome them. He might have helped Walt more if he had simply listened to his heartache and silently prayed for him.

Another aspect of listening involves the *appropriate sharing of our personal experiences*. It is usually *not* appropriate to turn conversations into detailed explanations of our own experiences. Few of us want to share our concerns with a person who patronizingly says, "I know what you mean. Why just last month I went through the same thing and . . ." and then goes on and on describing their own problems and solutions while we wait for them to return to and listen to our problem.

Thomas Bracken well stated the grief we heap upon ourselves and others when we fail to receive or give empathy and understanding:

> *Not understood!*
> *How trifles often change us!*
> *The thoughtless sentence or the fancied slight*
> *Destroy long years of friendship and estrange us*
> *And on our souls there falls a freezing blight;*
> *Not understood.*
>
> *. . . Oh God! that men would draw a little nearer*
> *to one another! They'd be nearer Thee,*

I Accept You, I Understand

And understood.

—Thomas Bracken
(from the poem "Not Understood"
in The Best Loved Poems of the American People)

Empathy and acceptance are two of the most effective ways of carrying out Christ's command to love each other as He loves. Acceptance lets others know they are accepted precisely as they are and empathy lets them know someone understands their feelings.

4

I CARE, I FORGIVE, I'LL PRAY WITH YOU

Carry each other's burdens, and in this way you will fulfill the law of Christ (Galatians 6:2).

Reading another of the apostle Paul's "each other" commands—to carry each other's burdens—reinforced our growing understanding that the catchy little phrase, "God is all I need," is quite unbiblical.

Studying the passage more carefully, we found the word *burden* refers to something so heavy and oppressive that it would cause its bearer to fall or stumble under its weight. Whether the result of our own or another's sinful pattern, or a circumstance beyond our control, a burden presses on our mind, causes us anxiety, and keeps us from growing more Christlike, more fruitful in the Spirit.

The heavy burden of resentment, for instance, keeps us from experiencing love. The burden of anxiety and guilt stifles peace. Depression kills our joy. The burden of anger robs us of patience, kindness, and gentleness. The fruit of the Spirit is grown, not by enduring these burdens but as we grow free from them.

Kindred Spirits

Others cannot help us until we are willing to take the risk of revealing our need. Burden bearing involves two or more people—one who shares his or her burden and another who will walk alongside, reflecting the Holy Spirit, the Counselor, the One "called alongside." Then the two walk together, bearing the same load, instead of one skipping miles on down the road leaving her friend alone and too weighed down to move.

One of Kathy's major burdens was her ongoing struggle to handle feelings of anger and resentment.

> When I realized what damage my anger was doing I prayed, asking God's forgiveness and for the power to control it. But before long I would find myself reacting the same way. Time and again I repeated this cycle. I grew more defeated. The answer to my prayers seemed so short lived. I sincerely wanted to change but my burden seemed too heavy. I began to wonder if one of the reasons my prayers weren't being answered was that I needed someone to help me.
>
> I called Alice and began sharing the depth of my frustration. It was easier to believe God wanted to help me with this burden when Alice demonstrated His care. Talking about my anger helped me understand why certain situations triggered it. For instance, I was most likely to lose my temper when I felt overwhelmingly inadequate to run my household up to the standard I had set for myself, or I'd get mad when I'd interpret my children's misbehavior as rejection of me as a mother. But my burden was lightening simply by the fact it was being shared and my new insight began melting away the fears and inadequacies which had for years contributed to my anger. As I obeyed the command to share my burden with others, I began to see God answer a prayer that seemed to have gone unheeded for years. One of the reasons things were different was that I was obeying God's command to share my burden.

Of course we cannot bear the burden *for* another but *with* another. Even though Jesus feels the full pain of sin's effects and has removed for us its hopeless sting, He usually does not magically remove our burdens from us, depriving us of our autonomy and responsibility.

Having a burden is similar to being a marathon

runner. For twenty-six miles you endure knots in your stomach, spasms in your intestines, and strained Achilles' tendons but you know you have to keep on running to finish. Someone else cannot run the race for you, but someone may run along beside you verbally or silently encouraging you, handing you cups of refreshment, helping you pace your journey realistically.

As we continued our times of prayer and sharing we learned it is nearly impossible to bear another person's burden if we have a similar burden of our own that is weighing us down. Alice remembers her struggle to help her teenage daughter, Kim, overcome her feelings of failure and rejection.

> When Kim felt rejected by anyone or any circumstances, she often responded by coming home and verbally lashing out at others in the family. Because I could not handle my own feelings of rejection I could not handle hers. I would leave the room or send her to hers until she settled down. But my reactions were simply adding rejection on top of rejection! I really couldn't be helpful to Kim because I felt too rejected myself.
>
> As I shared my own burden of fear of rejection, however, I found I could gradually separate Kim's pain from mine. I remember the culmination of my growth in this area. Kim was a sophomore in high school and ran for a school office. I wanted her to win as badly as she did, believing this would be a tangible way to build her confidence which had been shattered by a series of recent failures. I was also convinced a success experience would assure her of God's involvement in her life—something she had been doubting. The school nurse called me the morning of the election results asking me to come and pick up Kim because she was upset. My heart sank. I knew she had lost—another failure.
>
> *O God, how could You?* I thought. *Why did you let her fail again?* All the way to school I shouted tearful protests to God. When Kim got in the car we looked at each other and both began to cry.
>
> I will never forget the day we spent together, because for the first time I was prepared to really be *with* Kim in her pain. I didn't need to run or try to "fix her up" to avoid the hurt. I just tried to understand.

Kindred Spirits

That turned out to be one of the most important days of our lives. We talked about Kim's feelings and my feelings, and we talked about things we had avoided talking about for years. The election turned out to be a stimulus that uncovered years of hidden pain. And since I had faced my own feelings of rejection and had begun to know and accept myself, because others had accepted me, I could accept Kim's hurt. By the end of the evening, although the pain of her election loss was still there, we had found something much more meaningful. God knew we needed that bridge in our relationship far more than Kim needed to win an election. His love was tangible to Kim in a much more forceful way than if she had simply won an election. And He was able to communicate His love because I was able to bear Kim's burden. Both of us understood more deeply how Christ bore our griefs and sorrows, as described by Isaiah 53:4. Exactly a year later we saw another fruit of our time together. One of Kim's Christian friends went through exactly the same trauma at school. Kim was right beside her physically and emotionally sharing her grief and showing a new depth of concern and empathy—bearing her burden. Carrying each other's burdens is truly fulfilling the law of Christ—to love one another.

Confess Our Sins to One Another

Therefore, confess your sins to each other and pray for each other so that you may be healed (James 5:16).

By the time we studied this verse we were both finding it much easier to admit our faults to each other. But this verse made us wonder just how far we should carry confession. We had seen some people publicly proclaim their sins in an almost bragging way. We had seen others go to great lengths to confess minute, long forgotten offenses. And we knew other Christians who confessed their struggles, but only *after* they had "gotten victory" over their sin or solved their problem. Because we had seen so many approaches to confession, we decided to look for answers to specific questions about confession. *What* should we confess? To *whom?* and *why?*

I Care, I Forgive, I'll Pray with You

What Do We Confess?

James says we are to confess our *sins, faults*, and *offenses* so that we may be healed. In other words, we are to confess sins we need help in overcoming. If we have prayed about sinful attitudes or actions and continue in them, we need someone to whom we confess them, someone who can pray *with* us.

As we looked at our lives, we saw our sins fell into two categories—*offenses* and *defenses*. Our offenses were the conscious ways we hurt or sinned against others. Our defenses were the ways we protected ourselves from the anxiety of inner conflicts and difficult experiences. As we got to know ourselves better we found that our defenses were often the source of our offenses. Our sarcasm, pouting, or stubbornness, for example, were often defenses designed to "cover up" unacknowledged feelings of loneliness, rejection, or inadequacy. At first we hesitated to call these defenses sin. We wanted to label them "problems," "habits," or "normal emotional reactions." But as we studied Scripture we realized all of these were expressions of our sinful natures. They were clear evidence that we were not yet fully mature or conformed into the image of Christ. Alice had a real struggle in learning to call sin sin.

> When I first began sharing some of my negative attitudes and Kathy labeled them sin, I was enraged at what I perceived as an accusation. I argued, "How can you say that's sin? It's merely a fault or weak area." To this day I can hear her kind, gentle reply, "Alice, you must feel that when you admit any sin you are automatically condemned. Romans 8:1 says the Lord does not condemn you, and neither do I." Kathy's acceptance freed me to begin admitting that some of my problems were sin instead of fearfully hiding my offenses.

The more secure we felt in each other's presence, the freer we felt to confess specific ways we were sinning or attitudes that seemed to overpower us. The more sensitive toward sin we became, the easier it was to know *what* to confess. Looking more freely at sin did not lead us into morose introspection or depression or cause us to focus only on the negative things, because our confessions always effected forgiveness and eventual healing. Scriptural confession became a positive way of growing toward holiness. As we continued sharing and praying together we found ourselves confessing attitudes—judgmentalism, worry, and depression—as well as sinful actions, and as we confessed these we began to change.

To Whom Do We Confess?

What we confess often determines *to whom* we confess. According to Scripture, when we commit offenses we should go directly to the one we've offended. When we want understanding or help with our defenses, Scripture points us to a godly friend—someone who will listen with acceptance and be able to encourage and help us. Alice recalls how this process worked for her:

> Kathy was often able to help me see my defenses and how they influenced the offenses I committed. I remember one particularly bad week. I was uptight with myself while working on this book and taking out my frustration on the whole family. I was criticizing and demanding perfection from everyone in sight. Dick received the silent treatment because I didn't feel like being involved with him. And after Kent worked for two days polishing our car I still managed to find two places he missed! Kim wanted to practice driving before getting her license. I was impatient and nit-picked every stop and start, then I ended our excursion by saying, "That does it. You're not ready to get your license!" My attitude was wreaking havoc on our family life and I couldn't stand myself because of it.
>
> When Kathy called I told her of my verbal rampage. After listening she offered acceptance and insight into why my demands were so unrealistic. She didn't criticize me but heard both my hurt and the pain I was inflicting on everyone else. Her acceptance kept me from being defensive about my actions and gave me the desire to confess my problem to both the Lord and my family. I went first to the Lord and found myself spontaneously thanking Him for who He was and for forgiving me.

The next day I was fine but my family wasn't! I needed to confess directly to those I'd hurt! So I went to each one, asking forgiveness for the specific way I had hurt them. Once I did, they were understanding and eager to forgive. Communication was open once again and I was reconciled not only with my Father, but with my family, His children. The process involved confession to my friend, to God, and to those I had offended.

Why Confess?

James gives us the purpose of confession when he writes "so that you may be healed." While this may include physical healing, the primary focus is on the healing of sinful attitudes and actions. We confess, in other words, to promote our righteousness or "right living." The purpose of confession is not merely to ventilate our problems. Confession is not simply a kind of religious catharsis. We confess because confession brings honesty and healing.

Confession is essential to becoming righteous because it sensitizes us to the ever-present destructiveness hidden in sin and to the health and healing of living righteously. It helps us develop our discernment muscles. Paul prayed, "for I want you always to see clearly the difference between right and wrong and be inwardly clean" (Philippians 1:10 LB).

Confessing our sins to another person also keeps sin from controlling us. Satan hates light. He likes to remain unknown and hidden so that sin can secretly destroy. That is why most of us have a tendency to hide or isolate ourselves when we are struggling with sinful patterns. Unconfessed sin can even affect our bodies, as guilt and tension churn our stomachs and wrack our heads with migraines. David writes, "When I kept silent, my bones wasted away through my groaning all day long" (Psalm 32:3).

A friend of ours shared with us the effects of an unconfessed sin in his life. For a long time he had waged an

Kindred Spirits

inner battle with lust involving the wife of one of his friends. Every time these couples were together Keith would push aside the reality of his marriage and entertain fantasies of life with this other woman. She seemed to be everything he idealized. Then he found himself thinking about her when they were apart—day-dreaming. Knowing this was not God's will for him, his emotions and desires played vicious tug-of-war. The intensity of his passion shocked him, and his inability to overcome it was devastating. The more he prayed and tried to forget her, the worse the struggle became. His desire for this other woman stifled his love and concern for his own wife and left him frustrated and irritable. This went on for weeks, then months, until he lost his appetite because his stomach was always in knots. He longed to tell somebody of this wrenching, yet he kept it to himself because he thought his Christian friends would condemn him as much as he condemned himself. Eventually Keith wound up in the hospital with a bleeding ulcer.

While he was hospitalized one of his close friends visited him and Keith finally shared his inner torment. Surprisingly, his friend did not condemn him, rather, confessed his own similar previous struggle. They talked together and prayed for some understanding for Keith and for release from his lust. This was the first step toward wholeness. The confession began the process of healing.

Pray for One Another

> *The prayer of a righteous man is powerful and effective (James 5:16b).*

Prayer plays a central role in biblical friendships, and that role cannot be separated from our responsibilities to confess our sins to each other and to bear each other's

I Care, I Forgive, I'll Pray with You

burdens. Obviously we cannot know what to pray for unless there has been confession. And when we pray for each other we are helping bear each others burden's.

You have probably read or heard others read James 5:16. The King James Version says, "The effectual fervent prayer of a righteous man availeth much." But if you have been a Christian very long you have probably heard committed Christians fervently praying ineffectively. You may well have had the experience of confessing your sins to God, and sincerely, in all good faith, seeking an answer or a solution to a need in your life or the life of one you love, only having nothing happen. James 4:3 says that sometimes our prayers aren't answered because we ask with wrong motives. But frequently this is not the cause of unanswered prayer. When we repeatedly pray that God will change a sinful attitude, such as worry, resentment, or depression, we are obviously praying in His will. Yet frequently nothing changes. When this happens we either become upset with God for not answering or with ourselves for our apparent lack of faith. But this doesn't have to be! A closer look at James 5:16 tells us why.

Just before James wrote "The effectual fervent prayer of a righteous man availeth much," he challenged us to "Confess your faults one to another, and pray for another, that ye may be healed" (James 5:16 KJV). Many of our prayers are not answered because we have split this verse in two and only attended to the latter half. We pray, but we do not confess our sins to each other and pray for one another. Once again, our "you and me, Lord" approach to Christianity causes trouble. Gospel songs, such as "Tell it to Jesus Alone," contain great truths of God's care for us, but they tell only half the story. We also need to tell our struggles to God's children! Christ said, "if two of you on earth agree about anything you ask for, it will be done for you by my Father in heaven" (Matthew 18:19).

Kindred Spirits

Mutual prayer, based on an honest sharing of our needs, has power, and for several reasons. To begin with, it helps us define our needs, sins, and answers to prayer. When we confess our sins to a friend our specific need is often clarified. For example, we may want to present a prayer request that our husband or children will change. But in sharing our need we might begin to see that we are a part of the problem! Then we can pray not only for others but for ourselves!

Many of us have a habit of praying in general terms. We pray, "Lord, forgive my sins," without really being specific and facing them directly. Or we pray, "Lord give us a happy marriage," rather than "Lord help me overcome some of my nagging, my criticism, my anger, or my depression." Because sharing with a friend encourages more specific praying, it helps us see more specific answers.

When Kathy determined to learn to express her frustrations and opinions to Bruce without attacking him and to take responsibility for her part of any conflicts that arose between them, she went to Alice for support.

> I drove to Alice's house for the day knowing I had made a commitment to myself and to God. After catching up on all the latest events in each other's lives, having coffee, and laughing at some silly pictures one of her kids had taken, I began to tell her more details of a recent insight I'd had into the way Bruce and I handled disagreements. I was skilled at saying, "You are stubborn and make me mad." I was very poor at saying "I am stubborn. I am furious. I disagree."
>
> Alice had been around our family and had observed what I'd been explaining. She agreed with what I saw and encouraged my commitment to change. We prayed together. I remember how specifically she labeled the circumstances which make me most tempted to blow up, asking the Lord to help me take responsibility for my reactions and tone of voice and inner attitude.

Praying with and for each other is one of the most precious characteristics a godly friendship can have. The three way relationship that flows as two or more kneel before their Lord is a reflection of the Trinity itself and an answer to the prayer Jesus prayed, "That all of them may be one, Father, just as you are in me and I am in you. May they also be in us so that they may be one as we are one" (John 17:21).

5

I WILL COMFORT AND ENCOURAGE YOU

"Therefore encourage (admonish, exhort) one another and edify—strengthen and build up—one another, just as you are doing" (1 Thessalonians 5:11 AMPLIFIED).

Since we didn't think we should need anyone but God comforting and encouraging us, we never saw the great biblical saints as needing anyone either. Then one day we read 2 Corinthians 7:5–7, where Paul was lonely for his friends:

> For when we came into Macedonia, this body of ours had no rest, but we were harassed at every turn—conflicts on the outside, fears within. But God, who comforts the downcast, comforted us by the coming of Titus, and not only by his coming but also by the comfort you had given him. He told us about your affection, your deep sorrow, your ardent concern for me, so that my joy was greater than ever.

With new eyes we read old, familiar words. Here was Paul admitting he was depressed, anxious, and lonely. Obviously he had prayed for encouragement but it didn't come to him in some memory flash. It came through the presence of his dear friend.

Kindred Spirits

Encouragement for the Future

While the twin ministries of comfort and encouragement overlap, encouragement is the more future-oriented of the two. It focuses on strengthening and helping one another toward becoming more like our Lord, reminding each other, when depressed, of what we already know about the Lord. We encourage each other to hope, to press on in spite of our hard trials, and not to fear the future because His presence and promises are true.

Often we need this kind of encouragement from each other just before giving a seminar. One of us is bound to say to the other, "How can I possibly stand before others and talk about the Lord and my relationships when I feel distanced from God and am having trouble applying the principles I'm going to talk about?" The other is always ready with acceptance, understanding, and the encouragement of not forcing us to "get it all together" by the time we are to give the seminar. We know that our own inadequacies allow us to be fellow strugglers with those to whom we speak, which helps us empathize with them. When the day comes for the seminar we always feel ready to go because of the loving encouragement offered us.

In 1 Thessalonians 5:14 we could see more specifically how to encourage one another. Different people need different kinds of help—"Encourage the timid, help the weak, be patient with everyone."

The timid are those who find it difficult to live the Christian life in the face of opposition, who are not naturally bold, or who get overwhelmed by the stress of things. Encouraging these people means showing them plenty of support and love.

The weak are those who who often fail spiritually. We are to hold on to these, not despising them, but sticking with them, eventually bringing them to maturity.

I Will Comfort and Encourage You

We realized we are not totally weak people, yet each of us has weak areas such as anger or lust or anxiety, in which we easily fail. If we were not encouraged it is easy to condemn ourselves and feel "What's the use, I'll never change." But when others don't leave or give up on us but offer us acceptance and forgiveness and the hope that God has the power and the provisions to enable us to change, we are strengthened and our immature areas mature. Whatever form encouragement takes, its purpose is to strengthen us to endure and to press on toward Christlike maturity.

Comfort for the Past and Present

While encouragement looks toward the future, comfort helps us cope with present pain. When we've been shaken by illness, death, serious problems at home or work, a comforting friend soothes and helps us cope. Just hearing, "I'm sorry, it must be very painful. I'm standing by with support in whatever way you need," is sometimes all we need.

Kathy remembers meeting an old friend one day on a visit to the hospital:

> Jan's drawn face revealed the heavy strain she was under. A month before she had given birth to a mongoloid baby who was now very ill in an incubator. She could only stand beside it, watching helplessly, unable to even hold her child. I found myself wanting to share her suffering but having a strong urge to run from it because it brought up my own fear of having a mongoloid baby. Even though I felt uncomfortable being with her, because she was my friend and hurting, I stayed with her. I found myself first of all identifying with her shock at having an abnormal baby, then with the feelings of not wanting it, and with her searing question "why me?" For a period of time we met together weekly, then fear of losing the baby she'd come to love deeply became a reality, and we grieved together.
>
> Jan needed comfort as she learned to accept her baby, then, later, to accept her loss. In her deep despair, the only way she could tell that

Kindred Spirits

God was still there and caring for her, was that she knew He'd brought us together.

Sometimes we give help and comfort in practical and physical ways. Paul reminds us, "When God's children are in need, you be the one to help them out" (Romans 12:13 LB). When the Moores, friends of ours, were off in another state, offering comfort to their dear friends whose home had just burned down, their own home flooded with mud. When they returned and discovered the mess, they called two Christian friends. Within minutes at least twenty people arrived to help with the clean up.

Another family, new to the community, lost their little girl in a car accident. They had not lived in town long enough to develop close friends but the Christian community, hearing of the tragedy, visited, brought food, and undertook all the details they could. A neighbor, after observing this kind of comfort, sought the source and became a believer.

As we comfort one another we accurately reflect our Comforter, God, who in 2 Corinthians 1:3–4, promises His comfort will always be equal to our need. We have found that we feel least comforted when we isolate ourselves from other people. Because the Holy Spirit lives within Christians, we hamper the Holy Spirit's work when we distance ourselves.

A teenage daughter of another friend suddenly died. The father grieved for days by locking himself in his room, refusing to see anyone who came to comfort him. His wife and other daughters, grieving together, tried to get him to be with them, but to no avail. A friend who had recently experienced the loss of his teenager came by and sat in the living room waiting. After several hours the bedroom door opened and the father came out. His friend stood up, walked over with open arms, and said, "Come here. Let me

I Will Comfort and Encourage You

take care of you." With that the father sobbed like a baby in enfolding arms.

Months passed and death struck again within his church. Who was beside the bereaved? The one who had just been comforted.

When we don't have this tangible sense of God's desire to comfort and encourage us while under trial and stress, it is easy to doubt that He cares. If we continue to nurture our doubt, our trust begins to diminish until we become bitter and faithless. (See Hebrews 3:12–13.)

Kathy was shocked to find herself angry at God and doubting His care while temporarily living in Hawaii.

> One day while my mother was visiting, we took a long walk down the beach, stopping to pray. We specifically committed her safety and future to the Lord. But, later that day, at the airport she fell and broke her hip. The next day she underwent difficult surgery and was told she would not be able to walk on that leg for six months. I felt every one of the five thousand miles separating us. The only immediate thing I could do was pray for her as she went through the operation and faced the long siege of immobilization. Why hadn't He protected her as we'd prayed and how could I trust Him again? A tug-of-war began between what I knew the Word said about Him and what I felt. For several days I tried but could not change my perspective. The bitterness toward Him was affecting my relationship with Him. I knew I needed encouragement from someone who not only knew and loved me but was outside the situation and could be objective. That was Alice. Even though she was three thousand miles away, I called and told her my feelings. After she listened she gently helped me see that I was assuming that God was as helpless as I *felt*. In a loving voice she reminded me that God did care about me and my mother and that He would wonderfully redeem this experience for both of us. Her loving words melted my anger and renewed my trust in Him. She had helped make His strength and love real again, which brought me comfort and encouragement.

There are as many ways to comfort and encourage as there are needs and trials. Comfort may be an accepting smile or just sitting in the quiet presence of a trusted friend.

Kindred Spirits

It can come through Scripture, prayer, a warm hand, an understanding embrace. Sometimes it's the faith our friend has in us and in God's character that encourages us and enables us to rise to the high demands suffering and stress make on us.

6

I WILL LOVINGLY CONFRONT YOU

Be gentle and forbearing with one another (Colossians 3:13 AMPLIFIED*).*

Admonish those who are out of line (1 Thessalonians 5:14 AMPLIFIED*).*

In 1 Thessalonians Paul gives us one of the most difficult instructions to carry out. He writes:

> And we earnestly beseech you, brethren, admonish (warn and seriously advise) those who are out of line—the loafers, the disorderly and the unruly; encourage the timid and fainthearted, help and give your support to the weak souls (and) be very patient with everybody—always keeping your temper (1 Thessalonians 5:14 AMPLIFIED).

The first part of the verse, the admonishing, seems the most difficult to do. To admonish another is to give serious warning about his or her sin. This type of admonishing is directed toward people who are very much caught up in a destructive pattern of sin and are either unaware of it or unwilling to change. Notice that we are *not* told to admonish the timid, but to *encourage* them and to *support* the weak. Timid and weak people do not need stern warnings and admonition, but for the unruly, encouragement and support are not enough. They also need strong warning!

Most of us find it relatively easy to encourage timid people or to help the weak, but it is not easy to go to another person and lovingly point out their sinful attitudes or practices or unmet obligations. We usually find it easier to ignore these problems, to talk to someone else about them, to use excuses like "I'm not my brother's keeper," "I want to let him learn for himself," "Let God show her," or "Let someone else do it."

As Christians we may claim it isn't our responsibility. After all, we say, Matthew 7:1 says, "Do not judge, or you too will be judged." Actually this verse does not mean we are to ignore the sins of other Christians. It means we are to evaluate without criticizing or looking down on a brother or sister as being inferior. If we really care about our friends we will not want to see them suffer the results of sin. As with all of the "each others," the reason we admonish is to help our friends mature and become more Christlike.

Because going to another Christian and lovingly confronting him or her with a sinful pattern was such a rare occurrence in our experience, we carefully studied what Paul meant by this command. As we did, three important issues came to light: when to admonish, how to admonish, and whom to admonish.

Sometimes we hesitate to admonish a sinning friend because her behavior angers us and we sense we can't confront her in a loving way. At such times it is probably best to wait until our attitudes change or to let someone else do the admonishing. But often we don't admonish because we lack courage or fear rejection. It's easier or safer to ignore the problem!

When to Admonish

Our first concern was when to admonish. Were we supposed to run in and correct each other over every little thing as soon as we observed it? We hoped not, since this conjured up unpleasant pictures of spiritual busybodies breathing down everyone else's backs! We were relieved to discover that admonishing is to be preceded by forbearing one another. Paul speaks of "Forbearing one another, and forgiving one another" (Colossians 3:13 KJV). And Peter reminds us, "Above all, love each other deeply" (1 Peter 4:8). To forbear means to bear graciously offensive or sinful attitudes and actions of others, delaying discipline as long as possible in hopes that the person sees his or her own offense and does something about it. Many times, our loving acceptance and patience with another person is stronger than rebuke. We all need time to grow and discover our own offenses, and if others are too quick to point out our bad habits, quirks, or sins, they can create a climate of judgment, defensiveness, and discord. Before we rush in to admonish another person we need to provide a sensitive, mutually loving atmosphere of forbearing and patient forgiving. Only when this fails do we need to admonish.

As we forbear one another's faults we are reflecting the Lord, who is extraordinarily patient with us (2 Peter 3:9).

How to Admonish

The Bible gives some very clear guidance on how to admonish another person. This advice establishes a clear alternative to ignoring another person's sinful patterns or attempting to correct them in a condemning or judgmental way. In Romans 14:10 Paul tells us "You have no right to

Kindred Spirits

criticize your brother or look down on him. Remember, each of us will stand personally before the Judgment Seat of God" (LB). Paul says that we must conduct all of our relationships *uncritically*. God has given His children only one level on which to stand with each other—eye level. This leaves no room for attitudes of superiority or criticism which communicate condemnation rather than acceptance.

The second way we admonish is *humbly* and *gently*.

> Brothers, if a man is trapped in some sin, you who are spiritual should restore him gently. But watch yourself, you also may be tempted (Galatians 6:1).

The word *restore* used here is the Greek word used for restoring a broken leg. We shall help a friend caught in an ongoing sinful pattern with the same gentleness we would a broken bone. A sensitivity to our own weaknesses and need at times for similar help enables us humbly to approach a sinning friend. In fact, to try to "restore" a brother or a sister with any attitude other than gentleness and humbleness is to fall into sin ourselves.

As we admonish we must go *ready to forgive*. Jesus said:

> If your brother sins, rebuke him, and if he repents, forgive him. If he sins against you seven times in a day, and seven times comes back to you and says, "I repent," forgive him (Luke 17:3–4).

One of the best tests to determine our motivation for admonishing someone is to ask ourselves whether or not we have a forgiving attitude. Sometimes we would rather set a person straight or tell him off than forgive, but, at such times, we obviously don't have his or her best interest at heart. Trying to admonish someone when we have this attitude reflects more our desires to vent our anger than it does a desire to be helpful. Colossians 3:12–13 says that we are to clothe ourselves with compassion, kindness, humility, gentleness and patience. Bear with each other and

I Will Lovingly Confront You

forgive whatever grievances we may have against one another. Biblical admonishment can only be carried out from a personal concern for the welfare of the admonished, and therefore, we need to accept and empathize with the other, bear the other's burdens, and pray for the other *before* we admonish. These concerns form the basis of a meaningful relationship and give us the right to speak these most difficult words of correction.

Whom Should We Admonish?

Once we clarified the attitudes needed to admonish a fellow Christian, we found four main situations where the Scriptures indicate we should admonish or confront others about their sins. The first is *when our friend sins against us*.

> If a brother sins against you, go and show him his fault, just between the two of you. If he listens to you, you have won your brother over (Matthew 18:15).

Especially within family relationships, when we have been wronged it may seem most natural to fight back or withdraw. But neither of these tactics solve the problem.

For the first several years of marriage Dick and Alice lived more like parent and child than peers. If Alice felt wronged, she withdrew like a shrinking child.

> Dick is a very competent person who likes things done well. When he asked me to do something I usually rushed to do it thinking I was submitting to him. But after a while I began to resent the way he made his requests. It seemed commanding and I realized I was feeling resentful even though I still complied with the requests. I would withdraw and sulk instead of telling him how I felt when he spoke to me like a commanding officer, which only compounded the problem.
>
> We had been living in stony silence for two days and I wanted to reach out to him, so I fixed a special dinner hoping that would help break the barrier between us. But when Dick came home he noticed I had not finished two things he'd asked me to do, and he hit the ceiling. We sat down to eat, but I felt like a smoldering volcano. I just

Kindred Spirits

poked at my food. I knew I wanted peace between us and not a fight, but I knew it wouldn't do any good to ignore the problem because it would just come out some other way.

Finally I said, "I felt attacked and condemned tonight when you came home . . . more like your child than your wife. I'm sorry I didn't do what you asked, but I feel you were wrong in how you told me."

Much to my surprise Dick responded to my new tone and word message. He apologized and expressed his frustration at coming home and seeing certain things that were important to him unattended. Because he didn't attack me I could accept and feel his frustration. The resentment we both felt so strongly was gone. The last half of the meal was suddenly enjoyable!

That was just the beginning of changing a pattern between us.

Another situation in which we need to confront a friend is when he or she is *trapped in sin*. Paul writes:

> If a man is trapped in some sin, you who are spiritual should restore him gently. But watch yourself; you also may be tempted (Galatians 6:1).

Translated from the Greek, *trapped*, means *overtaken*. It is being caught off-guard by sin—unpremeditated sin. These sins are unconscious blind spots that we don't see in ourselves. The word *restore* implies a process that takes place over a period of time. We recently observed a beautiful example of this kind of confrontation. Nine-year-old Mike is a hyperactive child who, because of some physical difficulties, was highly restless, easily provoked, and had a hard time controlling himself. Consequently he needed tightly structured environment and loving, firm, consistent parental discipline. But Mike's father, John, found it easy to ignore Mike's outbursts or let his mother try to handle him.

One weekend while John and his wife were gone, Mike stayed in the home of friends. Mike acted as he always did, being verbally and physically abusive to the

I Will Lovingly Confront You

other children, not mindful of limits, generally out of control. When the friends lived with Mike's uncontrolled behavior they saw his need for limits and realized that his parents would have to set them. They also sensed how blind John had been to the seriousness of his son's problems. After discussing their concerns with another party to gain a second opinion, these friends decided to tell John what they thought was needed, and so they asked for an appointment with him. In the hours before the meeting John anticipated the seriousness of his friends' concerns. John later said, "I felt such a heaviness in my heart and body that I thought I would never be able to get up out of my chair to go meet them."

John's friends felt just as heavy-hearted but they proceeded to review their observations of Mike's conduct: He had verbally abused their daughter. Ten families in their church had complained of Mike's physical abuse to their children. Some of the children refused to be around Mike anymore.

It was a difficult experience, but John began to see the gravity of the problem and his need to exercise better discipline. Looking back John said, "I could see my son was *begging* for my love in his own negative way. The weight of what my friends said was heavy, but their attitude was so caring that I had to listen. I began to see the potential consequences if I didn't help Mike now, and their love and support enabled us to begin to take responsibility as parents. They even helped me see what I could do.

"First, I confessed my own inconsistency and asked Mike to forgive me. Then I pledged to discipline him until he learned limits for his behavior. As the days passed I consistently disciplined, hugged, and prayed. At first Mike resisted our discipline. Then a strange and wonderful thing began to happen! Mike started liking our new system and seemed to feel more secure. He was ready for our next

Kindred Spirits

step—asking forgiveness from the neighbors he had offended. We sat down with Mike and made a list and talked about how he could approach them. Then we prayed together. There were sixteen people in seven different homes on that list! As we walked into the cool autumn night, Mike said he was afraid. I told him I understood and that I was nervous too. My own pride was shaken by having to face the people offended by my own son. I assured Mike we would go together and that I would comfort, support, and love him always. Our first visit was humiliating, yet the forgiveness Mike received was a relief to both of us. In the next couple of weeks we sought out each person on that list and apologized. When they responded positively Mike began to gain confidence and feel more secure with his peers. One father even took the time to drop by and compliment him on his new attitude in the neighborhood.

"We learned a lot of lessons through that experience. Among the greatest was the demonstration of how our Lord stands by us always, even when we grieve Him. It was an opportunity to teach my son how Christ is concerned for his welfare. As Mike received forgiveness, he literally began to skip as he walked—the burden of his sin being lifted. You can't believe the change that's come in that boy and our family because our friends had the courage to 'tell it like it was.'"

Now the two families have an even closer relationship because they cared enough to follow Jesus' instructions, no matter how difficult the confrontation seemed.

A third situation in which we are called to admonish is when a friend *persists in a serious sin*. In 1 Corinthians Paul gives us some strong words:

> What I meant was that you are not to keep company with anyone who claims to be a brother Christian but indulges in sexual sins, or is greedy, or is a swindler, or worships idols, or is a drunkard, or

abusive. Don't even eat lunch with such a person. It isn't our job to judge outsiders. But it certainly is our job to judge and deal strongly with those who are members of the church, and who are sinning in these ways. God alone is the Judge of those on the outside. But you yourselves must deal with this man and put him out of your church (5:11–13 LB).

Evidently, the sins listed here are particularly destructive to ourselves and other relationships.

Sonja was involved in the destructive sin of adultery. "I felt as if my spiritual battery was dead! Oh, the Holy Spirit was still convicting me that what I was doing was wrong, but I just couldn't get things moving in God's direction. What's worse, I began moving in the opposite direction empowered by the force of sin—faster and faster. It felt exhilarating and exciting—like wind blowing in my face. I felt carefree and nothing else seemed to matter.

"Yet at night I would lie awake in the darkness and have to face the reality of what was happening to my life. The darkness of the night seemed a symbol of the darkness in me. Almost every night I'd cry and pray that God would help me find a way out of this situation. I knew there was a small spiritual spark still within me.

"I got up the courage to share what was happening with two close friends. One of them, Mary, has been one of my closest friends for several years and the other, Anne, had recently become a part of my life. They both just listened and encouraged me to get help. I felt their acceptance and knew they understood, but I resisted their help. Months later Mary called and said she and Anne wanted to come over. We decided on a time.

"When they came through the door I had the strangest feeling of wanting to run. I wished they hadn't come, yet I knew God heard my prayer and was now answering by sending these two friends. Mary's words were piercing as she said, 'I have searched the Scriptures and my heart and I

Kindred Spirits

believe God's Word says that to show my love for you I must break off our friendship. I even told the Lord that I am willing to die if it will cause you to turn to Him. I love you and care that much about you being lost.'

"Then she handed me a piece of driftwood on which she had written, 'For I am offering you my deliverance, not in the distant future but right now! I am ready to save you.' [Isaiah 46:13 LB] I read it and began to weep. I knew the time had come to walk out of the darkness into the light. I wanted to pray. Both friends moved beside me and put their hands on me while I prayed out loud. It was as if someone had put battery cables on my worn-out battery and plugged me straight into heaven! With the Holy Spirit in me it was as if God the Father and His Son were beside me. We three wept—I felt cleansed and knew that God had turned me around because I wanted to end this destructive relationship. After they left I wrote this man telling him the relationship was over."

We are to go to friends who are in conscious sin and ask them to stop. If they refuse, we are to bring in other caring witnesses, and, if they still refuse, we are to withdraw from their friendship until they repent. If they fail to repent, we are to take it to members of the church who are to put them out of the church until they repent. According to 1 Timothy 5:19–20 this same process is to be carried out with leaders of the church.

There is another situation which does not call for the stern rebuke of admonishment but calls for the courage to confront people about difficult situations. This is <u>*when a friend has something against us*</u>. Christ said:

> So if you are . . . offering a sacrifice to God, and suddenly remember that a friend has something against you, leave your sacrifice there . . . and go and apologize and be reconciled to him, and then come and offer your sacrifice to God (Matthew 5:23–24 LB).

I Will Lovingly Confront You

This scriptural injunction seems to be the opposite of our natural human response, "If he has something against me, let him come to me!" Yet Jesus clearly stated that if we remember that a friend has something against us, we should go apologize and initiate the reconciliation. It's as if *we* are asking to be admonished!

The picture, in context, is of an Israelite at the temple about to hand his animal sacrifice to the priest, who is going to kill it, then lay it on the altar of sacrifice, pleading God's mercy and forgiveness for all his sins. But just at the moment of transaction with the priest, the worshiper recalls a friend who bears a grudge against him. The worshiper may not bear a grudge, but if he thinks his brother has one toward him, he is to leave the service, go seek out his brother, apologize, and be reconciled with him, then come back and worship.

Jesus sees such a close connection between loving relationships with people and worship that He challenges us not to worship until we have made reconciliation! The apostle John stressed this point when he wrote, "If we walk in the light, as he is in the light, we have fellowship with one another . . ." (1 John 1:7). This principle is so important that Christ asks *us* to take the initiative to find out how we may have offended another person by humbly telling him or her we sense we have done something offensive. Then, if we have, we ask forgiveness.

The final situation where we are encouraged to go to a friend is *when there is an unresolved dispute*. Paul writes:

> If any of you has a dispute with another, dare he take it before the ungodly for judgment instead of before the saints? Do you not know that God's people will judge the world? . . . Are you not competent to judge trivial cases? Do you know know that we will judge angels. . . ? Therefore, if you have disputes about such matters, appoint as judges even men of little account in the church! I say this to shame you. Is it possible that there is nobody among you wise enough to judge a dispute between believers? (1 Corinthians 6:1–5).

Kindred Spirits

Paul strongly admonishes (rather than commands) Christians to take local grievances before qualified Christians. God places confidence in us, His children, reminding us that one day we'll be ruling the world and angels, making these earthly matters trivial by comparison. He asks us to find wise people within our midst, even those of little stature in the church, to help us settle our conflicts. There may be big conflicts, too, and the "wise people" may be a deacon board or group in the church.

We often act as "a third party" for each other when we feel we should go and confront someone else, but our anger or fear keeps us from going with a spirit of gentleness, humility, and readiness to forgive. We listen to each other, help each other gain objectivity and insight into the conflict until we are "armed" with helpful, rather than harmful, attitudes.

But we do not *always* rely on each other to be our "third party," as we have found it most helpful if the third party knows both the offender and the offended fairly well and will function as a peer rather than one whose suggestion must be followed. The role of this third person is to mediate, clarify, and be committed to both parties—not taking sides but helping each take responsibility and seek reconciliation.

This was a new concept for us and many in our circle of friends, and sometimes we've had to teach a third party what we've wanted them to do for us. For instance, we've said, "I'm very angry at my husband right now. I want to tell you how angry I am and I want you to listen and try to understand but not to take sides. Eventually I'd like to talk about what I can do to make our relationship better, but first I need to be heard."

Kathy tells the story of a committee meeting where her friend, Pat, was quite outspoken.

I Will Lovingly Confront You

I vehemently disagreed with what she was saying, yet I tried to put the lid on my feelings. However, that was like trying to box mercury from a broken thermometer. On the way home I stopped at a friend's house who knew both of us fairly well and I expressed my frustration. She listened empathically, then raised some questions about why Pat might be feeling the way she was. I left feeling understood and with some insight into Pat's feelings.

In a couple of days, Pat called. I felt nervous when I heard her voice, but after making our way through superficial topics we got down to the fears and misgivings about our relationship. We could offer each other understanding yet maintain our points of view, and that brought us to reconciliation. Later I found out that she, too, had gone to our mutual friend for help. Our third party kept our confidences, was committed to us both, and helped us gain perspective.

In this particular instance Kathy and Pat did not sit down with their mediator, but such a three-way personal discussion is often best. Two people in conflict need the physical presence of the third person because it's easier to say what one thinks and feels when one feels the safety of another person who will not be biased, especially when the conflict has been unresolved for a long time and strong feelings have built up.

Everyone needs to learn to say how she feels but never at the expense of someone else's feelings. Often the third person can help you say how you feel without attacking, or when you do attack, help you see how it might feel being at the other end of a loaded pistol. We have found this to be one of the most helpful aspects of friendship. It is easy to be blinded to another's feelings by the intensity of our own. It is at those moments that we can't feel empathy for a friend's struggle when we are furious at her. Our anger only blinds our ability to feel her struggle, to understand what she is going through.

Alice and Dick are dear friends with another couple who sometimes act as their third party. Their friendship

Kindred Spirits

has grown so close that Alice and Dick welcome Jim's and Rachel's help rather than fear it.

> One evening when we were eating out together Dick and I shared a recent, but repeated, conflict. They both listened, but it was Jim who lovingly spoke firm words, correcting me about how I was coming across. He expressed what Dick often feels, but somehow hearing it from Jim gave me the ability and desire to empathize with Dick instead of criticize him. This kind of commitment and support within our marriage has borne a phrase commonly used around our house when we have an unresolved conflict: "Go call Jim and Rachel and see if they can come over and listen."

Living within close, loving relationships in God's family makes confrontation seem healthy and natural. But when we live *outside* of any caring relationships, when we are not known by anyone else, we lose the safety of understanding. Without other people to lovingly mirror ourselves back to us, we are never sure how we appear to others; we never know how we have *misjudged* our appearance to others. We can't see patterns in our lives that are self-defeating until some harsh encounter is forced upon us or until we figure out the reason behind the silent rejection. Within godly relationships, however, we can feel loved rather than condemned, even when we are confronted.

God's Word says, "Look after each other so that not one of you will fail to find God's best blessings. Watch out that no bitterness take root among you for as it springs up it causes deep trouble, hurting many in their spiritual lives" (Hebrews 12:15 LB).

As we begin to lovingly confront one another God gives promises of blessing: "Whatever you bind on earth will be bound in heaven, and whatever you loose on earth will be loosed in heaven.... If two of you on earth agree about anything you ask for, it will be done.... For where two or three come together in my name, there am I with

I Will Lovingly Confront You

them" (Matthew 18:18–20). These promises immediately follow Jesus' own instruction on prayerfully exercising correction of each other. God has clearly delegated disciplinary authority to His children to be exercised for the sake of repentance and growth, never for justice and condemnation. It is meant to reproduce God's holy character within each of us.

7

YOU—GOD'S MIRROR TO ME

> *As I have loved you, so you must love one another. All men will know that you are my disciples if you love one another (John 13:34–35).*

As we incorporated these principles into our lifestyle, we became aware of some of God's great purposes in our relating to each other. We are to be like mirrors to each other of God's attitudes toward us. We can be mirrors that brightly reflect the glory of the Lord (2 Corinthians 3:18).

For instance, as we accept each other as Christ accepts us, we are teaching each other how God accepts us (Romans 15:7).

As we empathize with each other we reflect Christ, our High Priest, who is *deeply touched by our needs.*

> For we do not have a high priest who is unable to sympathize with our weaknesses, but we have one who has been tempted in every way, just as we are—yet was without sin. Let us then approach the throne of grace with confidence, so that we may receive mercy and find grace to help us in our time of need" (Hebrews 4:15–16).

Kindred Spirits

The empathic understanding of a friend helps us realize how deeply Christ shares in our struggles. It lets us know we have a Savior who does not let our cries "go in one ear and out the other," but who deeply and personally enters our lives. Our friends' understanding and unconditional acceptance help make God's grace real.

As we listen to each other's confessions and pray for each other, we reflect Jesus, our High Priest, who stands before God on our behalf reminding God that He has already paid the penalty for our sins. Jesus encourages us not to sin and confronts us with their terrible consequences, but He also speaks to His Father in our defense. When godly friends listen to our confessions and pray with us, they reflect a portion of Jesus' concern for us as well as His attitude of loving correction and forgiveness.

Our willingness to admonish one another lovingly, when sin is the issue, helps communicate God's concern for holiness and His attitudes of correction toward us, His children.

> God disciplines us for our good, that we may share in his holiness. No discipline seems pleasant at the time, but painful. Later on, however, it produces a harvest of righteousness and peace for those who have been trained by it (Hebrews 12:10–11).

Although it takes courage to confront sinning brothers or sisters, our willingness to do so can help them gain a deeper appreciation of God's holy character and understand that sinful living is destructive to their own and others' welfare. The light of God's holiness teaches us more about ourselves and our Savior!

We see these truths vividly demonstrated in Jesus' life. He was the perfect expression of His Father. He taught the Twelve about the Father, not just by communicating facts (Christ could have accomplished that in a few weeks), but through the relationship He had with them.

Paul, too, modeled almost everything he taught. He taught the churches doctrine regarding their relationships with one another and with God, but he also lived what he was saying. Paul relates:

> You yourselves are well acquainted with my manner of living among you from the first day that I set foot in Asia, and how I continued afterward (Acts 20:18 AMPLIFIED). We continued to share with you not only God's good news but also our own lives as well, for you had become so very dear to us (1 Thessalonians 2:8 AMPLIFIED).

Paul says he not only gave them the *gospel* but his own *life*. This taught them the truth that Jesus, God's Son, had given *His* life for them. Paul's faithfulness also taught them about Christ's commitment to them. He told his fellow Christians, whether I am in prison or free, I always pray for you, and only God knows how I long for you. (Philippians 1). Even in the midst of his own trouble Paul was concerned for them. He didn't pray for them as a religious duty or ritual but because he loved them and wanted them to grow.

Since God is invisible, we are the visible faces of His love. Just as Eve was a tangible expression of God's love for Adam, we are visible expressions of His love for each other. As we love and are loved we gain a deeper understanding of the reality of God's many-faceted love for us. The apostle John wrote:

> No man has at any time seen God. But if we love one another, God abides in us and His love is brought to completion—to its full maturity, runs its full course, is perfected—in us! (1 John 4:12 AMPLIFIED).

The accuracy of our reflecting is dependent on how well we know and live God's Word, which tells us what to look for in Him and in each other.

As we are faithful to Him by accurately reflecting to each other His attitudes, we can help correct distortions of

Kindred Spirits

Him, of ourselves, and of each other, that sin always causes us to have. When you feel cold and alone, shut away from the reality of His understanding and involvement—when that seems more real than His words of Scripture—a friend's caring and understanding can help bring you back in touch with the warmth of His true image.

Being finite and fallen we can only catch and reflect to each other tiny rays of His full-orbed, infinite warmth and light. Yet we are only helpful as we *reflect,* not try to *be,* the Lord's love to each other. In other words, our relationships with each other are not to replace personal relationships with God, only strengthen them.

Reflecting Each Other's Strengths

Not only can I reflect *God* to you, I can also reflect to *you* what you are really like. John Powell, in his book *The Secret of Staying in Love*, expresses it this way:

> It is an absolute human certainty that no one can know his own beauty or perceive a sense of his own worth until it has been reflected back to him in the mirror of another loving, caring, human being.

Even as our own eyes cannot see the face they're in without a mirror, so you cannot see what you look like inside apart from a friend.

What is it a friend can help you see? I can help you see your *strengths, your gifts,* and your *growth*. This happens as I encourage and build you up. Alice stayed at Kathy's home for a few days while working on this book.

> One night after a family dinner Alice mentioned to me some of the strengths she had observed at close range within our family: the closeness we felt for each other, the fun we had together, the way we as parents could instruct our children without condemning, the complement Bruce and I were to each other, and the deep contentment we showed in the other's companionship. At first I was shocked. My old picture hadn't adjusted yet to the new changes, until

she brought them into focus. Gradually my shock turned into deep gratitude. She had been God's loving mirror to reflect back to me the growth that had taken place.

Reflecting Each Other's Emotional and Spiritual Needs —

Not only can friends mirror each other's gifts, strengths, and growth, each can mirror the other's *God-given emotional and spiritual needs*. We can help each other recognize our God-designed need for acceptance, worth, and confidence. We cannot only help each other *recognize* needs but we can then *minister to them* because our needs are both brought out and healed by relationships. As we accept each other, bear one another's burdens, encourage each other, we minister to these basic universal needs, which are inherent in our humanity, as we were created for relationship with God and others.

As we honor each other (Romans 12:10), we minister to the other's need for a sense of worth. A friend can help you gain a sense of your own value and significance as a person created in God's own image.

The Bible teaches us we are all created by God (Genesis 1:26–27), gifted by Him (1 Corinthians 12:1–25), indwelled by the Holy Spirit (Ephesians 1:13), and that we should see ourselves as people of dignity, value, and significance (Psalm 8). When we lack a sense of self-esteem we tend to suffer from depression, guilt, lack of confidence, and a host of other emotional struggles. But when we see ourselves as God sees us, as His dear children, we gain a healthy sense of confidence and self-respect.

As a friend affirms you she ministers to your need for a sense of confidence in tackling the tasks and challenges before you.

God has not only made us with needs but provides godly ways for meeting them. As we discover the satisfaction of having our needs met in these ways, we can more easily resist the temptation of getting them met in ungodly ways.

Reflecting Our Weaknesses and Sins

Within Godly friendships we not only reflect gifts but in time, we may also reflect each other's weaknesses and sin patterns. Not by pointing them out, but by providing a safe atmosphere in which we see them for ourselves.

Sometimes an atmosphere of love and acceptance is created, yet a serious sin pattern persists or a serious blind spot exists. This was true in Sonja's situation. The love and empathy were not enough to help her out of the bondage that held her. She needed firm confronting about her persistence in her sin.

As Dietrich Bonhoeffer said in his book *Life Together*, "Nothing can be more compassionate than the severe rebuke that calls a brother back from the path of sin. Nothing can be more cruel than the tenderness that consigns another to his sin."

Moses—God's Mirror to Israel

Godly friendships are designed to teach us about God and about ourselves in order to promote our holiness. This realization reminded us of Moses, the man to whom God spoke "face to face as a man speaks to his friend" (Exodus 33:11 AMPLIFIED). We found that God's friendship with Moses was a rich example of the effects of godly friendship upon our understanding of ourselves and God, which in turn affects the way we treat others.

God's first encounter with Moses was in the wilderness where Moses had been shepherding for forty years. As Moses was walking along a bush suddenly burst into flames and a voice called out "Moses! Moses!"

"Who is it?" Moses asked.

"Don't come any closer," replied the voice. "Take off

your shoes, for you are standing on holy ground. I am the God of your father—the God of Abraham, Isaac, and Jacob."

God initiated his friendship with Moses by letting Moses know at once of his Holiness. What a strange way to begin a friendship, you might say. Yet showing Moses His holiness was one of God's greatest gifts and one of His deepest acts of friendship. True love and friendship seek the good of the loved one and cannot be separated from holiness since holiness hates what is destructive to the other's best. As the giver of all life, God sees sin as a slow death and He wanted Moses to know from the beginning that He had at heart Moses' welfare as well as the Israelites'.

As God continued speaking to Moses from the bush, Moses covered his face because he was afraid to look at God. Then the Lord told him:

> I have seen the deep sorrows of my people in Egypt, and have heard their pleas for freedom from their harsh taskmaster. . . . Now I am going to send you to Pharaoh to demand that he let you lead my people out of Egypt (Exodus 3:7, 9).

The very nature of the task God asked Moses to do reinforced the centrality of God's holiness since it demonstrated His desire to free His people from their bondage to the pagan Egyptian rulers.

The size of the task God gave Moses also revealed His confidence in Moses. But Moses certainly didn't feel much confidence! Showing the anxiety many of us have felt he exclaimed: "But I'm not the person for that job!" Showing complete understanding and acceptance of Moses and his doubt God responded, "I will be with you" (Exodus 3:11–12). But Moses protested, "They won't believe me!" "They won't do what I tell them to." "They'll say, 'Jehovah never appeared to you'" (Exodus 4:1). God did not discredit or belittle Moses like some of us might have been tempted to do. He already had trained forty years in the royal household back in Egypt. Without riding rough-shod over Moses' feelings of inferiority and insecurity, God held out to him the belief that he was the person for the job.

Moses saw himself as inadequate, somewhat like Peter, centuries later. Also, like Peter, he had unclear perceptions of himself and God. Moses did not really see God as strong enough to provide the help he needed and carry out the divine plan. Yet the Father showed the same patience His Son did with Peter. God stayed with him, listened to all his anxieties and excuses, and gradually led him to a place of confidence and trust.

To strengthen Moses' weak faith and build his trust, God gave Moses a sign. He asked, "What do you have there in your hand?" When Moses replied, "A shepherd's rod," God said, "Throw it down on the ground." When Moses threw it down it immediately became a serpent, and Moses started running! Then the Lord told him, "Grab it by the tail!" With much anxiety we are sure, Moses picked it up and it again became a rod in his hand! "Do that," God said, "and they will believe you!" God gave Moses a tangible assurance. And when even that didn't calm Moses' anxiety over his public speaking ability, God reminded Moses that it was He who had made Moses' mouth. When all this failed God gave Moses someone to do the talking—his brother Aaron (Exodus 4:2–16).

All Moses could manage to trust God for in this first encounter was a clear directive to go to Pharaoh. For now, this was as far as Moses could go. But God was patient with him, slowly helping Moses develop the trust in Him it would take to accomplish his task.

As God's friendship with Moses continued, God expressed His personal care to Moses and his people. He protected and defended them as He delivered them from the Egyptians and brought them through the Red Sea.

You—God's Mirror To Me

And He provided their food and water for over forty years while they traveled in the desert. Yet His care was not limited to the Israelites physical well-being. It extended to their emotional-spiritual welfare as well. Moses could bring their personal problems directly to God. He would go far outside their camp and set up a tent where he would meet God to talk about their problems. "As Moses entered the tent, the pillar of cloud would come down and stand at the door while the Lord spoke with Moses . . . face to face, as a man speaks with his friend" (Exodus 33:9–11). God's great personal care for Moses and his people moved God to come down and talk at eye level with His own created being about each individual's problems. And through this interaction Moses learned a great deal about his Lord.

Along with God's caring went His forgiveness. Time after time the Israelites doubted God's commitment and ability to take care of them. They accused Him of taking them into the wilderness to kill them. In their distortions of Him they forged Him into a golden calf—trying to make God into their own image rather than letting God make them into His. And they even threatened to kill His representative, Moses. Yet time after time, when they repented, God forgave their sinful disbelief and continued faithfully providing, guiding, and protecting them.

The impact of God's faithfulness and forgiveness on Moses was transforming, both inwardly in his attitudes and outwardly in his relationships with people. Insecure, fearful Moses became a man who greatly resembled his divine Friend. Having progressively understood God's holiness— His hatred for sin on the one hand and the glory of His goodness on the other—Moses was able to radiate some of that glory to the people, even though he, too, hated their sinful ways. Having experienced esteem and confidence from his God-Friend, Moses was able to carry out what seemed to be an overwhelming task.

Kindred Spirits

He was then able to offer esteem to the people by expressing confidence in them. "He chose able men from all over Israel and made them judges over the people—thousands, hundreds, fifties, and tens" (Exodus 18:25 LB).

Because God had remained faithful and committed to Moses, Moses was able to remain committed to the people. Having experienced God's continual care, Moses constantly assured them of the same, never doubting they would enter the Promised Land. Having experienced personally God's forgiveness for his doubt and then seeing God's continual forgiveness of the Israelites for their doubt, Moses deeply identified with God's costly forgiveness. He was even willing to pay the price of his people's sin by asking to be blotted out in their place so they could be forgiven (Exodus 32:32).

Through God's friendship with Moses, He not only transformed Moses, but miraculously carved out a huge nation, governing and guiding it. All God's laws and counsel were communicated through this friendship, and through it He equipped Moses to be a unique leader-friend to the people and to bring about great changes in their lives.

This story gives us a clear picture of the significance God gives friendship, and we can see that holiness is a hallmark of that friendship. Today, as His children, our friendships must bear the same imprint.

Being entrusted with the privilege of helping each other see more clearly who God is and who we are is a great responsibility, indeed.

How gracious God has been to give us His guiding Word, with its models and instructions. How gracious of Him to enable us to personalize what we read through one another, in whom He dwells.

One day we will no longer need each other's reflecting, for we shall "see Him as He is"(1 John 3:2), fully gazing on all the facets of His glory.

Yet as we are able to experience some of the reality of His love now, we will be better prepared for that meeting of Him then. And when, face to face, we discover how great His love for us has really been, we will fall overwhelmed at His feet. We will be able to look back then at the friends He gave us, those who caught and reflected some of this reality to us, with infinite gratitude. What a preparation and privilege He's entrusted to each of us today.

"We can see and understand only a little about God now, as if we were peering at his reflection in a poor mirror; but someday we are going to see him in his completeness, face to face. Now all that I know is hazy and blurred, but then I will see everything clearly, just as clearly as God sees into my heart right now (1 Corinthians 13:12 LB).

Let us go after our inheritance and His gracious provisions for us. Let us reflect to each other the glory of God's esteem for us, the goodness of His character, the depths of His caring. Let us affirm to each other every glorious ray from the Son which we see slowly added, caught, and reflected in each other's life.

— *Part Two* —

WHAT GODLY FRIENDSHIPS WILL MEAN TO ME

8

HOW DO I FEEL?

Somehow both of us grew up with the impression that knowing ourselves was not important. In fact, we had heard injunctions like "Only glance at yourself but gaze at God" so we often wondered if we should pay attention to ourselves at all! Understanding one's feelings or emotions was sometimes pictured as a nuisance. Positive feelings were a good but not necessary ingredient of life, and negative feelings were highly undesirable.

Denying Our Feelings

When we had negative emotions like fear, anger, or depression we thought we should somehow be able to change them immediately or make them go away. We both heard other Christians give advice like "Don't worry," or "It's wrong to feel that way," or "Stop being angry." But neither these commands nor our own efforts to change our feelings altered these emotions for long. Consequently we often felt like failures and responded by feeling guilty. We could, however, change our actions on command and we

Kindred Spirits

often followed the commonly heard advice: "Do the right thing regardless of how you feel." But that was not the cure-all. It just produced more guilt because we felt two-faced. We were acting one way while feeling quite another. We knew the Lord looks within our hearts to our motives and attitudes, so we were not satisfied with this external solution. We knew it smacked of the legalistic, fear motivated superiority of the Pharisees to whom Christ said, "You are like whitewashed tombs, which look beautiful on the outside but on the inside are full of dead men's bones and everything unclean." (Matthew 23:27).

Even asking the Holy Spirit to take control of our lives didn't instantly change our emotions. When we felt angry, for example, we asked the Holy Spirit to make us feel loving. But because we didn't understand the selfishness, fear, or pride behind our anger, this really didn't help. Now we can see we were really begging the Holy Spirit to sidestep our responsibility. By asking Him to instantly stop our anger we were trying to avoid the necessity of "exercising self-control." It was as if we were asking the Lord miraculously to remove a portion of our personality rather than helping us understand ourselves so we could grow and change over a period of time. But if God worked this way He would simply be creating a batch of computerized people acting, thinking, and feeling what He wanted. They would perform properly, but they would not be unique persons who respond of their own free will to His love and leading! Kathy remembers what used to happen when she tried to handle her negative emotions in this way.

> In addition to trying to pray away my strong feelings, I tried to control my emotions by increasing my Bible reading. I piled up passages that told me to put away wrath and to be loving and kind. But the higher my pile of verses, the higher my pile of guilt! Each new verse just made me feel more uptight with myself which, in turn, fueled my critical attitudes toward others. When fellow strugglers shared their

problems I did more preaching than loving listening. My sincere attempts to handle my negative emotions were increasing the very problem I wanted to resolve!

Over a period of time we began to find answers to these struggles. Growth is a process that takes time and we do not need to condemn ourselves because we don't have instant spirituality. We found that the Greek word translated *perfect* in some versions of the Bible actually means *mature*. It was used in Christ's day to refer to a fully ripened fruit. This meant that we shouldn't expect ourselves to change overnight by applying a set of spiritual formulas. We also learned that our *inner emotional lives are important to God*. The first three fruits of the Spirit are emotions of love, joy, peace. Without a rich emotional life we cannot experience and express these fruit of the Spirit. Jesus exemplified this, as His life reflects nearly all of the emotions we experience, including anger. While His anger was not in self-defense or retaliation, He did experience strong anger on several occasions. He did not just "think anger" when He saw the money-changers in the temple, nor did He "think pain" when He was misunderstood by His disciples. He *felt* the pain that comes from being the object of others' mistreatment and this enabled Him, as our High Priest, to be merciful and faithful and touched by the "feeling of our infirmities" (Hebrews 4:15 KJV).

Emotions are necessary and a valuable part of being a human created in God's image. God has strong emotions and has made us as emotional beings so that we can respond to His love and reflect it to others. *He wants us to feel and experience life emotionally, not just comprehend it intellectually!* He wants us to have spontaneous, personal reactions to people, things, and experiences.

Kindred Spirits

Hiding Our Feelings

As we saw how important our inner lives are to God we also realized this was the area of ourselves to which we could be most blind. Since we had been taught for years that certain feelings should be done away with, we had learned a large number of devious ways of hiding them. For instance, when we were angry, we could deny the fact that we were angry, but start to see how angry our husbands were. Or, if we were afraid of our sexuality, we could keep a good distance emotionally from other men. If we were worried and anxious, we could label it "concern." If we had been hurt by ones we loved, we could push aside our desires for tenderness as though they really weren't there at all. We were always trying to avoid fearful or upsetting emotions. But the result was that we shut out entire areas of our lives—failing to develop some of our positive emotions out of fear, and not growing beyond our negative ones because of guilt! People cannot really mature unless they understand themselves and their emotions.

This was the experience of Ted, a brilliant young college student who was having trouble convincing his girl friend, Ann, he loved her—and all because it was difficult for him to express his feelings.

Ann felt Ted was "nice" but more like a nice machine than man, and she couldn't respond with more than mild feelings of friendship.

Ted hadn't been able to feel much emotion within any relationship, with the Lord or his friends. Even the experience of leading others to Christ left him joyless. But it was his relationship with Ann that brought his problem into focus.

He told us what life was like at home, where "You could have done better" was a constant theme. The approval he longed for never came, so he found he could

How Do I Feel?

deaden the pain of never feeling accepted or approved of by locking his emotions into a tiny compartment, keeping them secretly stored. Consequently he learned to repress negative *and* positive emotions. Feelings are all one package.

We know we are not to act on all our feelings or verbally express our every emotion. The Bible does not support the selfish, impulsive, and popular lifestyle portrayed by the motto: "If it feels good do it!" God gives us—His children—the freedom to explore our feelings and value them, but through His Word He also gives us the security of knowing His perspective. God has declared what He's like, how He feels toward us, and what is best for us. This is *biblical reality, and* it is truer than even our strongest feelings. We may feel depressed and worthless but God's Word reminds us of the truest reality—that God has created and redeemed us and that He cares deeply about us despite the fact that we temporarily *feel* quite different. Some people may *feel* good in a homosexual or extramarital sexual relationship, but biblical reality can bring these feelings into God's perspective by offering the hope that He has more constructive ways of meeting our needs for love and understanding.

The lifestyle of Godly friendship helps us learn to see and value our positive emotions and constructively to restrain and grow out of our negative, immature ones. With acceptance and understanding comes the capacity for real and lasting change.

How Feelings Begin

As we realized the importance of our emotional lives we decided to take a look at the origins and importance of our emotions. Where do they come from and how can they become so problematic? We learned *that feelings are born and developed in our first experiences with people* —parents, siblings, relatives, and friends. God's first plan was that we should come into this world through a family of two parents. They were to be a *visual aid* to us of God our Father. Even before we could understand Him with mature minds, we were to understand emotionally and experience some of His personal attributes. Through our parents we were to experience what it's like to belong, to be accepted, to be valued and esteemed, and to experience a sense of confidence. As babies this occurs as we are cared for and cuddled. When our basic emotions are fulfilled, we subconsciously feel, "My needs are gently and wisely met," "I am never abandoned or alone," "I belong to two people who are committed to me and love me."

In an atmosphere such as this, it is easy to learn to trust and happily obey, to respond with a warm, happy feeling about ourselves and other people, and to respond with outward confidence and inner contentment. Since we are secure and loved, we can return this love to others. But with the entrance of sin into the human race this first experience of love and worth and security was seriously marred. Our responses were also marred. A perfect environment was now more the solution for us than it was for Adam and Eve. Although some parents give many more nutrients for emotional-spiritual growth than others, no set of parents can give perfectly and no child can respond perfectly. Consequently, by the time we reach adulthood, we all have a variety of destructive as well as constructive emotions and response patterns.

Since feeling patterns develop from our earliest relationships, they cannot be commanded to change instantly. We cannot command worry, depression, and anger to disappear suddenly. Why? Because, over a period of years, they were developed and reinforced through unhealthy relational patterns. In the same way we cannot command trust, joy, peace, and love to appear instantly, for they too are slowly grown through healthy relationships.

How Do I Feel?

This process even impacts our relationship with God. Have you ever considered how our understanding of many biblical commands, such as trust, yield, submit, and love, is filtered through our experiences with parents and significant others? For instance, there is a strong connection between our ability to trust God and our past experiences with trustworthy or understanding people. It is easier to trust God to be a good provider—if we have learned to trust our parents to meet out needs. It is difficult to trust God to provide for our emotional needs, if our parents didn't understand or fill such needs when we were small. If our parents were often too busy to listen and play with us, we might feel that God is to busy to concern Himself with certain details of our lives; we might feel guilty about taking up His time! If we, as children, felt our parents were weak and ineffective in providing strength and support, we may, as adults have trouble believing in the power of God to help us in a crisis. Or if submission and control in our families meant giving in to a parent's selfish anger or insensitive demands, we may find the idea of submitting to God or of allowing the Holy Spirit to control us a very uninviting possibility! If we learned to value ourselves only when we performed up to others' expectations, or if we were dependent on the capricious approval of moody parents, or felt constantly rejected, it may be difficult for us to experience "living under God's grace," unconditionally accepted.

If we have any of these deficiencies, we have the scars of painful unmet needs and we tend to develop a distorted picture of ourselves, of God, and of others. We fail to gain an accurate understanding of God's character because we transfer our concept of our earthly parents onto Him, and we fail to understand ourselves and others because we learn to repress both our painful emotions and the positive ones our parents had difficulty accepting and expressing. This can easily result in us going through life on four cylinders instead of eight. We try to live the Christian life without a deep understanding of ourselves or our Creator!

God Meets Our Needs

Fortunately God has a solution for this dilemma. He has provided us with a second family into which we also enter by "birth." In this second family, the family of believers, we can find healing for the hurts not met by the first. Here the distortions of ourselves, of others, and of God as my loving "Father" can be corrected.

This began for us as we accepted each other, listened to each other express previously forbidden feelings, and empathized with the other's underlying pain. Our mutual encouraging, comforting, confronting, and praying made it safe to share our burdens and confess our sins, where our past attempts to change through "instant prayer" or Bible reading or service alone had failed. We found this God-ordained process helping us learn to understand ourselves and to change our negative attitudes and actions. It was through this process of fulfilling the "each others" that we found the Holy Spirit was increasingly controlling us— and not by magically tapping us with instant loving feelings in answer to a quick prayer. We never dreamed of the healing power and maturing that would come as a by-product of this biblical lifestyle.

9

DO WE DARE?

"Everyone needs a friend like that, but do I dare?" responded one woman after hearing these principles. She was excited about the possibility of having a truly biblical friendship, yet she was aware of the risks and potential obstacles.

In our journey we discovered the existence of both external, or cultural barriers, and internal barriers, or personal anxieties about the implications and risks of getting close. As we "walk" through the obstacle course with you, we hope to break down the fear that might keep you from trying it for yourself.

External Barriers

One barrier to friendship is our *society's loose regard for commitment*. This is typified by a T-shirt motto we saw: "Sworn to fun, loyal to none." But are we happy with such loose connections? In the April 1981 issue of *Psychology Today*, sociologist Daniel Yankelovich says that, while nearly all Americans claim to have many acquaintances, 70 percent admit they have few close friends, and they identify this as a serious void in their lives. Over 40 percent revealed they have fewer close friends than they did in the recent past.

In the absence of deep friendships it is easy to understand why so many couples live together out of wedlock. One writer says this generation of young people is characterized by a belief that intimacy is dangerous and that the way to live safely is to reduce one's vulnerability to the low level required for survival. The parents of this generation find their commitments eroding too—as the rising divorce rate testifies.

The media has helped this erosion by offering a *make-believe substitute for real relationships*. One flip of the selector provides instant vicarious relationships! How many people do you know today who are more committed to their "soaps" than to their friends!

This tendency to avoid deep and lasting friendships and commitments is also encouraged by the *mobility* of our society. Never have we been able to go so far, so fast, so often. This mobility and the rapid urbanization of America has led to a "stewardess-syndrome," where we warmly smile at strangers as if we had shared the intimacy of a lifetime, then quickly pass by. Our frantic pace of life and the "instant mentality" of our advertisers further compound the problem. We get so busy running from one activity or appointment to another that we become accustomed to throwing a warm-up meal in the oven or stopping at a drive-through instead of sitting down together for a meal. If we are not careful we can start hurrying from one activity to another without ever taking time to really get to know the people we spend time with every day. This even happens in our families—especially when children enter adolescence.

It's a struggle, living in this world and not being *of* it,

Do We Dare?

keeping these trends and attitudes from weaving their webs within our living patterns.

But the trends of secular society are not the only ones we have to deal with. Some barriers are unique to our Christian culture. For some reason many of our churches have slipped into patterns or Christian viewpoints that also interfere with godly friendships. Because these attitudes are endorsed by "our own" they can be even more difficult to overcome than those growing out of the larger milieu.

The first Christian barrier is the *belief that God intends to meet our needs solely through prayer, study of His Word, and our Christian service.*

All of the "each others" validate the truth that He intends that our needs be met through godly relating *as well as* through studying His Word and praying.

Our needs are not met through service; instead we freely serve as our needs are met. The more whole we become, the more we want to offer others our love, concern, and care. When our needs are being met we are less vulnerable to the temptation of giving in order to get something back. When we're sure of our own acceptance we don't need "proof" from someone we're helping or reaching out to. We don't give mixed messages when our motives are not mixed so we're not disappointed by the results when our expectations are mixed.

The second barrier is the *tendency to value service—over piety*.

Do we place more emphasis on what we do for the Lord than on how we are like Him?

God's primary goal for our lives is that we mature into His image and His attitudes (see Ephesians 4:13). And doing so involves looking within ourselves at areas needing renewal *and* looking outward for ways to serve Him. We must not exclude either. If we only "give out," keeping busy in His service by running from one area of ministry to another while seldom looking within at our own needs and feelings, we will probably eventually crumble or fold. If we become so caught up in becoming inwardly Christlike, spending most of our waking hours in holy introspection, worrying about ourselves and others' piety, we will probably have little energy left for looking at the needs of others.

It's becoming openly apparent that service isn't always a barometer of a person's Christlikeness or wholeness. We've discovered leaders who walk around storing up anxiety, camouflaging depression, and hiding immorality. Eventually, when the dam bursts and a divorce is announced, a homosexual confesses, the despondent is hospitalized, the shocked Christian community wonders what went wrong.

It's a tragedy when our leaders don't seek closeness in mutual godly friendships or are denied the intense caring that is offered the more obviously needy. Some leaders may want to maintain the impression that they don't need to receive, and some congregations may need to believe that fallacy in order to protect their own idealistic worship of their leaders.

The third barrier is *valuing service over relationships*. Commitment to people must supercede "just getting the job done." When we value people only for their contribution to a project or ministry we actually *devalue* them. We may find it easy to commit ourselves to projects and goals, to want these successes so badly we ride roughshod over people's feelings. Sometimes beneath successful programs we can find battered relationships or church leaders who've become "program specialists," asking for our talent, money, attendance, and energy primarily to help them meet their goals, instead of to meet one another's needs.

Christian commitment means more than just helping one another perform better within a ministry, exercise

Do We Dare?

"gifts," or lead people to Christ and then moving on. It means sticking by others as they grow at their own rate, not just until they reach some sort of predetermined spiritual plateau or until they've finished some set of study books on Christian living. We discovered this means being committed to others even when they fail, sin, withdraw, regress, or become stubborn or unmotivated. Mutual commitment is to last as long as any family ties—forever. It is a measurement of our commitment to Christ.

When we forget that our love for Him is not measured and increased by harried service, Martha-style, but by the quality of our relationships with Him and each other, Mary-style, we need Jesus' gentle indictment to Martha: "You are worried and upset about many things, but only one thing is needed" (Luke 10:41–42).

The fourth barrier we face is that *Christian commitment is said to be to Christ alone.*

Scripture reminds us that we who do not love our friends whom we can see, cannot love God whom we have not seen (I John 4:20).

If we are committed to Christ then we are to be committed to His children. Our relationship with other Christians is meant to be a visual measurement of our commitment and love to Christ (John 13:35). He doesn't want us to come to Him with our "I love You's" if we remember a friend has something against us and we haven't tried to be reconciled (Matthew 5:23–24).

We live out our commitment to Christ as we fellowship (1 John 1:7), lay down our lives for our friends (1 John 3:16), and carry each other's burdens (Galatians 6:2).

The fifth barrier we confront is *we have needs only when we aren't trusting God.*

At one time we hid our feelings whenever we felt depressed or troubled, while outwardly maintaining a smile. Smiling could make it look as if we had constant spiritual victory and that the Spirit was in control while in fact we were camouflaging our discouragement. Admitting weakness or defeat would be admitting Christianity wasn't working the way we thought it was supposed to. Appearing needy didn't seem a very accurate likeness to Christ or a sign of our confidence in His sufficiency.

Admitting need seems like admitting immaturity. After all mature Christians appear to be less needy than the rest of us "young" saints. Yet many strong-appearing Christians, like this minister's wife, are crying inside for some tender care:

"I feel like a cement monument—with people leaning on me on all sides. I must never crumble or show need of repair. My husband is so busy that sometimes I feel guilty if I try to lean on him. I love our people and yet I am so lonesome."

It can take a long time to see how much we Christians confuse neediness with sinfulness. We are needy when our basic God-created physical, emotional, or spiritual needs are not met. Needs are created by God to be met in God-ordained ways, and we should never try to hide them.

The sixth barrier, especially for full-time Christian workers, is the *belief that we should be equally close to everyone in the church*. This usually means we keep a safe distance from everyone, for we cannot be close to all. But we need to follow Jesus' model of closeness and not try to be like the Holy Spirit who is equally close to everyone. Jesus loved everyone but He had a limited number of close friends. Jesus knew the multitudes, but He was intimate with twelve, closer to three, and closest to one! We do not need to apologize for having a small number of close friends, rather, we should actively encourage this. God has someone for each of us. This is God's desired provision for everyone.

Do We Dare?

Being close to a few can be a problem to those who are not part of that inner circle. Jealousy surfaces, especially by those who are lonely and want you to be their close friend. We need to take the same risk the Lord did without abusing the closeness.

This principle has freed us to become close to the few God has placed in our lives instead of spreading ourselves out like a thin coat of paint. And giving and receiving love with an intimate few equips us to love with greater depth others who are not as close to us.

The final barrier we may encounter is the idea that *our marriage partner should fulfill all of our emotional and spiritual needs.* Both of us entered marriage with this belief. We were confident that the man we had married could fill all our needs and that we could do the same for him. But were we in for a surprise! We soon found out our marriages *revealed* as many needs as they *filled*. Yet for several years we kept looking to our spouses and demanding they meet all our needs. This just loaded us all with guilt and frustration since we were demanding the impossible. This is not to say that our marriages don't help meet our basic emotional, physical, and spiritual needs. They do, as they should. Some people's greatest source of healing is their spouse. But we also need to look to other members of the body of Christ—to our friends—for strength and encouragement. This takes the impossible demands off our spouses and allows us to give more freely to each other because others are enabling us. At the same time a goal of friendship is always to strengthen marriage and never be a substitute or detriment to it. The January 1982 issue of *Christianity Today* cites research by Daniel Levinson of Yale which indicates that difficult adjustment periods for marriage partners, such as midlife crises, are more successfully navigated when each spouse has close friendships of his or her same sex.

Kindred Spirits

All the "each others" were given to everyone and modeled in relationships beyond marriage by Peter (who was married) and other apostles. Single people do not need to wait until they are married to enjoy the emotional intimacy that comes with biblical friendships.

Inner Barriers

This next set of barriers is more difficult to overcome. These are the barriers erected because of our own anxieties and fear. In his book *The Secret of Staying in Love*, John Powell wrote that "the most universal fear of all men is to be found out, to be known, then to be rejected." The highest of all hurdles to close friendships is surely *the fear of getting close to another person, allowing them to know us really well, and then rejecting us or turning against us*. Nobody likes to be rejected and as long as we keep a safe distance from others we have nothing to fear.

Kathy can speak to that point well.

> My way of keeping a safe distance was built in when Alice and I began meeting. Alice lived thirty miles away. Our monthly get-togethers and occasional phone calls were all I wanted. In fact, the thirty-mile distance between our homes was a good safety factor for me because the thought of having a friend close enough to "drop by" panicked me. I wanted to control our friendship by seeing Alice only under certain conditions. I felt very comfortable when we were praying about our ministries. I also felt comfortable when I was helping Alice or when she helped me in certain areas. But I felt insecure about just doing fun things spontaneously with people. I had grown up on the mission field and wasn't comfortable with others unless I was making a significant contribution. I also didn't want Alice dropping by unless my house was well in order. In short, I felt comfortable serving or even telling Alice about some of my failings or problems, but I was not the least bit excited about her actually observing my struggles. Thirty miles away was a perfect distance!

Closely related to the fear of letting someone know us well enough to hurt us is the fear that we will gain a friend only to lose her.

Do We Dare?

There is a desire to hold on to those we grow to love. Once relationships are established and flourishing with love there is that longing to keep things just as they are—forever. The sense of belonging is so satisfying—especially when God's love is being shared.

But in reality, people move on, even die, and we are often left behind.

This can be a real problem for those whose jobs require periodic moves. None of us want to leave the ones we love and some people decide this possibility is too big a price to pay for friendships. Consequently they settle for a variety of acquaintances instead of one or more close friends. This is understandable but unfortunate because we end up cutting ourselves off from potential growth and support. Alice remembers when her fear of being left by two very close friends became a reality.

> Phil and Nancy were part of a group of six with which we met weekly for four years. We had laughed and prayed together and shared some of the most meaningful experiences of our lives. I will never forget my feelings as we said good-by. We wound down their narrow street, toward their house, a bit slowly, trying to delay the inevitable. From a distance two yellow blinking lights on top of the moving van signaled the pain ahead. Until then I had neatly tucked away the pain of separation, but our friends' move was reality. The little white and yellow house once scrubbed and cozy and filled with good smells and tender love was now the scene of scurry and disarray. People packing and lifting, vacuuming and crying, coming and going, and taking with them stacks of tangibles that either didn't fit or were given to them as remembrance.
>
> I had only allowed momentary vignettes of our meaningful times with Nancy and Phil to cross my mind since the day they had announced, "We're moving to Oregon!" God had brought me so much of His love through these dear friends. They were with me as I struggled and were significant to the healing of some of my emotional distress and encouraged my spiritual growth. Their leaving symbolized the end of a season—one of the most painfully happy in my life. There would be new experiences and friends but never just like them. I wanted to

Kindred Spirits

cling to the past—the future seemed empty. As the four of us stood at the door, staring at the floor to avoid each other's eyes, the pain of love brought tears of grief. We all embraced like a vine and cried. Then someone softly responded, "Thank you, Lord."

That night and the next day the pain was wrenching, as if someone had died. I hadn't grieved for the loss of living friends before. This day I cried as memories of love faded in and out. As in death, the good memories tended to envelop the conflicts. I felt the cost of loving because I had given a part of myself away. But although our parting was difficult, I wouldn't trade those years with Phil and Nancy for anything. We still manage to share frequently by phone or letter or on vacation, and they will always be close friends, even though they aren't nearby!

A year after this loss came another. Jim and Rachel, the other part of the group of six, moved to Seattle. Dick and I went through the same grieving process as we adjusted our lives to their loss.

Though miles have parted us, something remains: God's intangible gift of friendship built within us. Something eternal and intangible—inner strength, inner comfort, inner peace, inner joy—developed through godly relating. It took the removal of their tangible presence to realize the depth and strength of the intangible gifts that remained.

Another frequent barrier to building deep friendships is the fear of conflict. In any close relationship we have to face differences of opinion. In our several years of friendship we have had a minimal amount of conflict—partly because both of us feared it! Even though we have shared very deeply in many areas, we have tended to avoid any possible conflicts for fear of destroying our friendship. As we were working on this manuscript, one of us brought up the fact that she had been feeling resentful because she felt she had been doing more than her share for several months. But as it turned out, we both felt precisely the same way! We had both kept our feelings to ourselves and harbored some resentment because we feared an honest discussion of our feelings might hurt the other person or come between us. But just the opposite was true. Once we could get the problems out in the open, we worked it out and our relationship was strengthened.

Do We Dare?

Another barrier is *the fear of losing control* of our emotions. Many of us fear closeness might stir up some deep feelings that we don't want to share or are afraid we might act on. Crying, depression, anger, and sexual feelings can make us think twice about developing close friendships because these feelings can be frightening and embarrassing. The key to overcoming this barrier is to choose friends we can trust with our thoughts and feelings, friends who are committed to our welfare as revealed in the Scripture. When we enter friendships with a keen awareness that they are given by God for our growth toward holiness, we will work to model both His loving acceptance in our times of struggle and our commitment to help each other live righteously.

Scripture says we need brothers and sisters, but many of us are uncertain how God intended those friendships with the opposite sex to be actualized. We need to see healthy, God ordained ways of relating to the opposite sex.

If we can keep a deep spiritual foundation alive, we can help each other become holy. Then tender situations can be made helpful and healing rather than enticing and uncomfortable.

Sometimes our fear of losing control of our sexual feelings is brought out when we are with those of our own sex. This emotional stirring and stress is a sign we need further understanding of our feelings so we can not only control them but heal them. When we don't understand these feelings we may either fearfully withdraw from the relationship or find ourselves under certain circumstances losing control—the very thing we feared.

As our own friendship developed we discovered one more barrier to the godly friendships we saw outlined in Scripture. This barrier was the *tendency we both had to avoid being peers or equals*. Initially one of us felt more comfortable sharing her needs or struggles while the other felt more comfortable in the "helper" role. Alice recalls:

Kindred Spirits

> I was so busy giving out at my church and in other relationships that I really needed someone to listen to me for a change and help me with my struggles. Since Kathy was a good listener and always seemed to offer good advice or help me come up with some new insight, our relationship began to fall into a pattern of one needy person meeting with one strong helper. Before long, however, we began to realize this was limiting our relationship.

And Kathy saw the same situation from a different perspective:

> There was a certain gratification and sense of worth I received from having Alice need me. Her appreciation also meant a lot to me. But gradually we realized this helper-helpee relationship was causing problems. It was really a bit dishonest on my part because I was acting as though I didn't have any very significant needs of my own. I had reached a point where I could just help others! Needless to say, I was kidding Alice and myself! Rather than encouraging her to see herself as a person who had something to offer me, I was reinforcing her tendency to think of herself as someone who had to have a parent figure to help run her life. Maintaining a helper-helpee relationship was also cutting off my potential for growth. All my life I had found it easy to avoid facing my own needs and feelings of weakness by appearing strong and helping others. Not until I could break the pattern of always being the helper could I receive some help I needed. If we had continued our relationship on this basis we would have cheated ourselves out of the process of becoming healthily interdependent and would have left one of us the chronic leaner and the other always the counselor or giver.

This pattern, of course, didn't change overnight. It took time to learn to catch ourselves falling back into our old habits. But as we became sensitive to our tendency we were able to work it out. This does not mean there are not many times when one friend takes on a distinctly helping role. In fact, that is just what the biblical "each others" are all about. The point is that these roles should shift within the friendship so that each person feels free to take the helper or the helpee role depending on the need. Whenever one person dominates the helping role it tends to set that

Do We Dare?

person up as superior and the other as inferior. This works against treating each other as peers and short circuits the process of growth.

As friends we need to be two people discovering Christ together, standing at eye level equally in the need of the Lord's redemption and grace, seeing each other as both gifted and needy. This biblical perspective of each other creates a safe emotional climate in which we "serve one another" (Galatians 5:13) and "be subject to one another" (Ephesians 5:21).

Serving each other is another way of expressing God's love. It means freely undertaking any task or commitment necessary or helpful to another's spiritual, emotional, or physical welfare. It may even be menial such as Jesus offered when He bathed the sore and dirty feet of His followers, or it may be offering empathy, bearing a burden, comforting. But however we do serve in His spirit, we make His love tangible.

We also make His love real to each other as we submit to each other. We are to be adaptable to each other in working out decisions, solutions to problems, and in accepting instruction. Keep in mind that this is quite different from obedience, which is something that can be demanded or coerced. Submission in this biblical sense must be freely and voluntarily given. It is self-imposed out of humility and the desire to serve. It cannot be demanded. The motives to be submissive can only be healthy when the choice is coming from a strong sense of worth and identity in Christ. Then it will not be submission out of fear and a slavish desire to please. It will reflect that characteristic of Christ so contrary to human nature, "who, though he was God, did not demand and cling to his rights as God, but laid aside his mighty power and glory, taking the disguise of a slave and becoming like men" (Philippians 2:6–7 LB).

You may not encounter any of the barriers we have

Kindred Spirits

faced, but you can be sure Satan will put some roadblocks in the path of godly friendships. He would love to have you limp along as a Christian lone ranger or as a person with many nice acquaintances but no one who really knows you well.

10

LET'S BEGIN!

Some of you have been reading these pages and saying, "I've got a friend like that! But I've never fully realized the value God gave our friendship."

Others of you may not have the close friend we've been talking about, yet you inwardly long for one who can experience with you the loving qualities of godly friendship.

But you're wondering, *How do I get started?* Some deep friendships grow out of longstanding acquaintances while others come out of brief chance meetings. Every friendship is unique, and the process of uncovering things we have in common with another person makes finding a new friend a serendipitous experience. By looking and listening sensitively for people we would like to get to know better, we can often find potentially good friends. Alice remembers the beginning of her friendship with Rachel.

> I was praying to find a new friend within my church community because I wanted to experience the same quality of friendship I had with Kathy with someone who lived close enough to me to be

Kindred Spirits

involved in my daily life. I was sitting in Sunday school one morning when I heard a woman speak up in a discussion time. We had never met but as she talked I listened intently. I heard words coming from her heart that felt as if they were coming from mine. I liked how she appeared but more than that, her sharing revealed an honesty and depth that made me want to get to know her.

Soon after that we both attended a couple's retreat and became acquainted. We talked right away about recent personal experiences and found we had much in common—a gregarious nature, similar types of involvement with people, husbands whose personalities were very similar, and both of us had similar backgrounds that had raised the same types of questions within our minds. We found we had common experiences and common voids within our lives.

Reach Out!

As you reach out, be prepared for possible disappointments. Some friendships just don't click. Not everyone is eager for this kind of friendship. This does not necessarily mean you reached out inappropriately or that you're not a nice person to be around! It may merely say others don't yet recognize the same needs you do. They don't want what you want, or they are too afraid to become friends and let you get to know them.

Once you meet someone you think you would like to know better, don't be afraid to reach out. Let that person know you are interested in becoming better acquainted. While this probably isn't the time to tell someone you are looking for a "best" friend, you can let her know you would like to have coffee and get to know her better.

Some people find the possibility of close friendship scary, but most would like at least to taste some of the fruit of a godly friendship.

Sally, a friend of ours, prayed to find a friend in her church. One woman she'd always admired kept coming to mind. But Sally had never reached out to her because she felt too threatened by her wealth and beauty. Sally saw her

Let's Begin!

several times after she had prayed and thought about her, but each time was too scared to initiate anything more than a *hello*. One day they came face to face in the mirror of the church women's room. After a few remarks Sally finally said, "I'd like to get to know you better. Do you think we could have lunch?" The other woman got tears in her eyes and said, "I've prayed for one year we could get better acquainted, but my personal problems have kept me too withdrawn to reach out."

Share Personally

Once you reach this point you can begin to share more personally about your interests, needs, and growing edges. It takes time to build trust, and most relationships move gradually from the stage of acquaintance to true friends who discuss personal concerns and spiritual pilgrimages. We have found different levels of trust within friendship. Discussing ideas, information, theories, and generalizations takes the least amount of trust. Sharing experiences from the past needs a little more; present problems and feelings require even greater trust. Sharing negative feelings toward each other in the present seems to take the greatest amount of intimacy and trust.

As you share, you will discover who really wants to grow in each of these three areas—in knowing herself, knowing God, and knowing you better. If you want to grow in any one of these areas and the other doesn't, your level of sharing will be affected.

This is also true of a small group situation. If three friends are meeting and two of the group wants to grow in all three areas and one is hesitant about growing in one area—say maybe in getting to know herself—the level of sharing will not exceed the openness of the most reticent one.

As we shared with others we found we needed to be

Kindred Spirits

sensitive not only to our own level of trust but to other people's as well. We also needed to test how much we should disclose. Jane, a friend of ours, had been abused by her father, and her past experiences affected her relationship with her husband and son. She trusted Sue enough to share with her these past details, wanting Sue to empathize and understand her. But it was hard for Sue to listen because she had had similar destructive experiences herself. Sue gently told Jane she could only listen to her general experiences, not the specific details, because it stirred up too much of her own pain from past rejection. As Sue slowly grew stronger and experienced more healing in this area, she could listen more deeply to Jane.

It may seem natural to give advice and probe when others express problems or troubling feelings, but, unless our friends want this kind of help, our questioning may come across as forcing them to tell what they may not be ready to share, which causes resentment and interferes with the development of trust and friendship.

Have Fun!

Helping each other with our burdens and struggles is not the only purpose of friendship. We all need relaxed, fun times together, and this is especially important early in a friendship. Recreation and laughter have a way of relaxing and refreshing us, and they also build strong bridges for our friendships.

Kathy remembers one particular expedition that helped cement friendships.

> A still photo of laughing faces reels off into living color as I recall our apple party. Three dear friends and I took off for apple orchard country exhilarated by the great music of Vivaldi's "Four Seasons" which matched the autumn colored panorama through which we were driving. We entertained each other with our own original musical scores too!

Let's Begin!

Selecting and tasting the variety of fresh-picked apples, enjoying the hikes, and conversing over our hot apple pie filled us with a desire to make it all last longer than one day. Inspired, we planned an "apple party," enlarged our group, and shared our bounty—apple pie, cake, bread, cider, and a pumpkin filled with spice pudding.

A knock on the door was from none other than the Great Pumpkin himself—all made up and rounded out carrying a sack full of gifts for each one. Pumpkin carols followed apple dunking and more photos—to record the uninhibited joy such fun with dear friends can being.

When we enjoy one another, we reflect an often overlooked attitude of God's—His pleasure and delight in us!

Finding Time

One of the hardest parts of maintaining a friendship is finding time when both or all people can meet. Scheduling sometimes takes more time than the actual get together! There are varying factors that influence time schedules from month to month, or week to week. Jobs change, commitments change, children grow older and our parental responsibilities change. Since there may be many people we must consider as we make time for friendship, we must be flexible while we maintain our commitment to be together.

Sometimes this can mean sacrificing sleep in order to have an early morning breakfast together on the spur of the moment. When schedules are more rigid, we need to agree on a specific time, perhaps every Tuesday lunch, or breakfast on the first Wednesday of each month. The specific purpose might be set—to share a burden, do a certain Bible Study together, pray for a shared concern.

To make room for friendship we may need to re-examine priorities. How do we spend our time? Who is important in our lives? God's priority is people. We in the body of Christ are to be number one on each other's lists of priorities. We are to "do good to all people, especially to

Kindred Spirits

those who belong to the family of believers" (Galatians 6:10). Kathy remembers trying to find time for regular involvement with friends.

> Trying to add time with friends to my already busy schedule was like trying to stuff a small envelope with an oversized batch of paper. Sometimes the envelope tears from the pressure. Between our church community, ministry, two children, a lot of entertaining, and other family responsibilities, I just didn't see how I could find any time for new or deeper friendships even though I knew the Bible said I needed them! Could this mean I was in for more guilt and failure? Finally I decided to make a priority chart to help me see exactly where I spent my time and energy, so I could determine what I could eliminate, add, or rearrange. If God said we needed deep friendships He could help me find the time. I listed the most important people in my life—my family and closest friends. Knowing our ten-year-old Dickie needed more time alone with me so he would know he is special, I worked out a regular weekly afternoon to do something fun together and give us time to talk. Under "Other Relationships" I listed other friends or acquaintances I would like to get to know better or with whom I wanted to keep in touch. After this I listed most of my other responsibilities and obligations. Then I sat down and prayerfully considered my whole lifestyle and its priorities.
>
> I found there were some things I could eliminate (like spending a lot of time with many people, instead of concentrated time with a few) and other things I could cut back on a bit or combine with other responsibilities. Bruce and I love to eat, for example, so it wasn't too difficult to make meals into special times of communication. Even telephone times had to be scheduled to ensure freedom to talk without infringing on the needs of family. Once I was clear about God's priorities for me, I didn't have nearly the struggle of knowing how to say "no" to some otherwise perfectly good involvements. I simply decided I was going to value the most important people and responsibilities in my life and not let other things interfere! This eased my guilt and conflict over saying *no* and enabled the Lord and me to be in control of my time instead of being controlled *by* my schedule. As I look back now I can easily see the rewards for setting my priorities straight. Because I have regular special times with Bruce and our children each week, we get along a lot better and know and enjoy each other more. They are my dearest friends of all. And because I found time for Alice and a couple of other close friends, I

Let's Begin!

have people who are supporting me in my Christian maturity and growth and vice-versa. All of this ends up helping to meet my own and my family's needs and enlarging my capacity to reach out to others. To my surprise I have also found I am getting more accomplished and have more energy than before.

Friendship Arrangements

As we begin developing a biblical quality of friendship we need to keep in mind that *the forms of friendship are flexible*. While the Bible gives us a lot of practical instruction on how we are to help each other, it does not tell us how many close friends to have, how frequently we should meet, and whether or not we should spend time as individuals, small groups, or couples. Both of us have had close friendships, one to one, with couples and within small groups. We have found all of these have contributed to our lives in unique ways.

The most intimate relationships are usually one to one. Sharing as couples has the valuable dynamic of two people coming together representing one unit, meeting others doing the same. Since God ordained the marriage relationship, few things can be more rewarding than sharing and praying together as couples who are mutually committed to each other's growth. Group sharing is usually the least intimate. Some find it easier to open up with several friends than with one person because they view such a situation as less threatening. Others don't feel free to share in group situations because they don't feel comfortable talking with more than one person.

Every person is unique and God does not expect you to force yourself into someone else's mold. He does, however, know that we all need more than superficial relationships, and He wants us to develop the quality of friendships that will allow us to minister to each other and be channels for communicating His love. We can look

Kindred Spirits

forward to beginning friendships knowing that God has some very significant lessons and experiences in store for us, but also with the flexibility that acknowledges His sovereignty and His desire to work in us as He sees fit.

The Velvet Friendships that Help with Sandpaper Relationships

We all have known family or friends who bring out the worst in us instead of the best, rubbing us at just the wrong spots, uncovering our weaknesses rather than our strengths. They're like sandpaper. It is good to remember that Jesus encountered these sandpaper experiences at times even from within His inner circle. It is also good to remember that one of His close friends was one He knew would never understand Him and would even betray Him. He was a constant sandpaper to Him, yet He loved him daily as He did the others. Even in this way He was laying down His life. Since we are also loved sacrificially we are to lay down our lives for each other (1 John 3:16).

But the Lord gives us others who are like velvet, whose words are comforting and supportive, and who really understand us. They are the soft cushions we need when we are scraped with the "sandpapers" and can listen to us as we explore the weaknesses and needs they bring out in us. They tangibly reveal God's perspective—just when we most need it.

Quality Time

Now that we have scheduled the time and chosen the people, what do we do when we are together?

There may be three questions you might want to ask yourself about the quality of time you spend together. First, do you spend profitable times discussing Scripture and spiritual issues without disclosing feelings and struggles? Do you do a lot of talking about yourselves, but rarely

Let's Begin!

discuss your problems within a spiritual framework, or do you get to neither of these areas? As you think about developing a godly friendship consider the balance of sharing meaningful Scripture and spiritual issues as well as disclosing feelings, struggles, and accomplishments.

Lasting Commitment

Even when commitment within friendships lasts, intensity within friendships can change.

Friendship is one way we reflect God's commitment to each other. The intensity of His commitment to all that is best for us and to meeting all our needs is constant, but the way He tangibly reflects His commitment to us and the people He uses in our lives changes.

Intensity within our friendships changes but we can remain committed to our friends—wanting what is best for them and being willing to be used by God to meet their needs as He wills and we are able.

God knows our limitations and what each of us can do and be. We must recognize and accept our own limitations as we try to meet others' needs, and others' limitations as they try to meet ours. It helps to be able to acknowledge openly and lovingly our inability to help each other in ways we wish we could. This dissipates feelings of abandonment when a friend can't help us, or feelings of guilt when we can't help another. If we face the fact that we can't meet anyone's every need, we won't be as tempted to "friend hop" when a friend can't help us. Just because we can't always help each other doesn't mean we are no longer friends or that we are no longer committed.

Our communities can only be strengthened as we take seriously our Lord's command to love each other as much as He loves each of us. In this way we will experience personal healing for our broken hearts and the transformation of our characters. Our testimonies will be far more

Kindred Spirits

convincing to a hurting world if we wear this mark of biblical distinction. As each of us reaches out to another, we will build up and strengthen the whole body of Christ, helping each other experience the reality of His healing, costly love. In this way we bring Him joy by obeying the command He so lovingly gave us. "Love as I've loved. . . ." We need to share this with the world, realizing as we do that we're not only fulfilling the Great Commission—"Go ye . . ."—but also the Great Omission—". . . teaching all things I've commanded."

Here is a letter from one whose friend reached out and loved her with Christ's love:

> Sue,
>
> I just want to say thank you again for loving me. I need your love in my life to strengthen me. Words cannot express what my spirit feels and knows because of your ministering to my needs. I feel uniquely blessed of the Lord because you really care about me. Praise be to God for showing me His lovingkindness through you. This strength that you give me is not of temporary or momentary benefit. This kind of strength is from God, our Savior, and it is enduring. Even if I never saw you again in this life, that strength that you have planted in me will live on and grow.
>
> God has used you to break the barrier surrounding me and keeping me aloof from others. Only God's love, through someone (you) could have ripped that veil in two.
>
> Believe me, you have been the key person to touch me that I might touch others. And so the ripple moves onward and outward to hundreds of hungry souls. Your reward for this in heaven and in this life will far surpass your wildest expectations and dreams.
>
> Use this special gift of loving others more and more, moment by moment, person to person! God is excited about you and what He's going to accomplish through you.
>
> I'm excited too . . .
>
> Your friend eternally,
> Linda

Even though we don't know you personally we know you are created uniquely by God for friendship with

Let's Begin!

Himself and others. May these ripples move out and touch you so you, too, will be able to use your special gifts of loving others as He loves you, moment by moment, person to person. We are excited about what God is going to accomplish in and through you as you grow in love toward your friend, yourself, and your loving Lord.

Alice and Kathy

Kindred Spirits

PRIORITY CHART

The Most Important People in My Life	What Our Relationship Needs	What We Enjoy Doing Together	Barriers
1. Bruce	Time alone for communication	Dinner alone weekly	Conflicting schedules
2. Dickie	Individual attention	Weekly date for fun and sharing	Letting other activities interfere
3. Debbie	Individual attention	Weekly date for fun and sharing	Letting other activities interfere
4. Alice	Opportunity for mutual spiritual and emotional growth	Regular time for prayer and sharing	Frequent schedule changes
5. Nancy	Opportunity for mutual spiritual and emotional growth	Regular time for prayer and sharing	Frequent schedule changes

ALL MY OTHER RESPONSIBILITIES AND RELATIONSHIPS:

1.
2.
3.
4.
5.
6.
7.
8.
9.

Study Questions

Here are some questions to share with a friend or small group.

Chapter One

1. Share your own spiritual journey.
2. Name the people who have influenced you the most on your journey.
3. When does it seem you need other people in your life? When don't you?
4. How do you feel about sharing your personal struggles with others?
5. In what way would you like to grow spiritually and/or emotionally?

Chapter Two

1. How could Christ's pattern of closeness with the disciples be reflected in your friendships?
2. What kind of friend was Jesus to John and Peter? What were His attitudes, reactions, and actions?
3. Could you identify with any more of John's or Peter's struggles?
4. What do you think caused Peter and John to mature?
5. In John 13:34 what provision has God given you to mature?
6. What do you think makes a friendship godly?
7. What are two purposes of godly friendships? How have you experienced these?
8. What ways can we use that Jesus used to teach his friends about God?

Chapter Three

1. Describe the time another person's acceptance became most real to you.
2. Describe the time God's acceptance became most real to you.
3. In what area have you struggled to accept yourself or another?
4. With whom do you feel most understood? What does that person do that makes you feel that way?

Kindred Spirits

5. Which is easier for you to share, your joys or sorrows? Which is easier for you to hear?

Chapter Four

1. How does feeling accepted influence the way you share your burdens with others?
2. How do you feel about bearing another's burden?
3. What problems, weaknesses, sins, or needs exceed your own strength and repeatedly cause you anxiety or guilt or anger?
4. How do you think bearing each other burdens fulfills the law of Christ?
5. Why do you think we are asked to confess our sins to each other as well as the Lord?
6. What needs to be confessed to each other? What are the guidelines? What are the precautions?
7. To whom do you confess?
8. How is confession related to effectual praying?
9. When has praying with another been effective in your life?

Chapter Five

1. How are you experiencing 1 Thessalonians 5:11 (LB): "Encourage each other to build each other up"? Whom do you encourage? Who encourages you? In what area does encouragement mean the most to you?
2. Read 2 Corinthians 1:3,4. How have you experienced God's comfort and encouragement recently? Can you explain the difference between the inner comfort of the Holy Spirit and the outer tangible comfort given by people? Since God is the Source of both, does one way seem superior to the other?
3. Read 1 Thessalonians 5:14. Have you seen these nouns and verbs mismatched? Explain how.

Chapter Six

1. How do you balance "admonish one another" with: "Don't murmur against each other" (James 5:9)? "Don't speak evil against each other" (James 4:11)? "Don't bite and devour each other" (Galatians 5:15)? "Don't lie to each other" (Colossians 3:9–10)?
2. How do you balance forbearing and admonishing?
3. Discuss any experience you have had of admonishing or being admonished. How did you feel?

Study Questions

4. What fears do you have as you think about being admonished? As you think about admonishing another?
5. How would you respond to being admonished? From whom would you accept admonishing?
6. As you admonish, what principles in this chapter would be most important for you to keep in mind?
7. What is the vital benefit of biblical admonishing to the church? What results when it is missing?

Chapter Seven

1. What helps make the Bible come alive to you?
2. Think of one of your friends. What characteristics of the Lord Jesus does he or she reflect to you?
3. What did you learn about godly friendships from the life of Moses? What was the hallmark of that friendship? What other characteristics of God did Moses begin to resemble?
4. What have you learned about yourself and God through your godly friendships?

Chapter Eight

1. What were your reactions to your parent's way of handling your basic needs: belonging, acceptance, worth, confidence?
2. How might your conclusions and reactions have carried over to your relationship with God? With other people?
3. How might God use your "second family" of Christians to meet these needs and correct negative patterns of reacting? When might God *also* use professional counseling?
4. When you hear biblical commands, such as trust, yield, submit, and love, how do you feel? Which is the hardest for you to do? Why?
5. What can we do when our emotions seem stronger than biblical reality?

Chapter Nine

1. Which of the secular external barriers affect your life?
2. Which of the Christian cultural barriers affect your life?
3. What does true Christian commitment include?
4. What impact can godly friendships have on marriages?
5. What significance can godly friendships have for singles?
6. Which of the internal barriers are hurdles for you?

Kindred Spirits

7. How did Jesus' friendship with the Twelve affect His discipling of them? How does mutuality fit in?
8. What motives liberate us as we submit to and serve each other? What motives put us in bondage?

Chapter Ten

1. Do you know someone who would like to grow along with you in these three areas of wanting to know God, yourself, and each other better?
2. How can you find time for your godly friendships? What will this do to your present priorities?
3. Why do you think the sharing of your personal struggles and joys in a scriptural context is important to godly friendships? What happens if you have one without the other?
4. What does this mean to you: "Commitment lasts but intensity within friendships can change"?
5. What results can come from remaining committed to your family and friends?
6. How does Christ's command to "love one another as I have" relate to His great commission in Matthew 28:19–20? What are you to teach? What is the best method?